TIRADES AND EVIDENCE OF GRACE

SUSAN BRIGHT

Photos by Butch Hancock

✳ Austin Book Award, 1991

ISBN: 0-911051-58-9
Library of Congress Number: 91-066434

Thanks
to the following people
for help
with this book:

Glee Ingram, Gerry King, John C. Andrews, Daryl Andrews, Helen
Schlegel, Mike Morgan, Elaine O'Brien, Betty Sue Flowers, Butch
Hancock, Tom Giebink, Karla Andersdatter and John Aielli.

Support for this book was granted in part by the City of Austin and Texas
Circuit through the Austin Book Award program.

PLAIN VIEW PRESS
P.O. BOX 33311
AUSTIN, TX 78764
512-441-2452

TABLE OF CONTENTS

THE METHOD

Of poetry
written in the first person
it is not essential that it be autobiographical,
just that it be true.
Thus we have a way of being
one might call,
the Experimental-I.
Existentially,
this is the life of the imagination
blended somehow
with the I-of-self
and integrated
by conventions of magic
and of art
into something
more true
than a single person's
experience.

TIRADES

ROLLER COASTER

For half a century
Poetry was the paradise
Of the solemn fool. Until I came
And built my roller coaster.

Go up, if you feel like it.
I'm not responsible if you come down
With your mouth and nose bleeding.

Nirancor Para

FOOD
GLORIOUS
FOOD

PIANO

for George Cure Bright

I am my grandmother's piano.

Grandmother,
the musician who would not allow
dancing,

Grandmother,
who insisted that the children
read, every morning and evening,
verses from the Bible,

Grandmother,
whose house was the town library,

Grandmother,
who wore pant skirts, calf length,
collected antique musical instruments
and fed us steak for breakfast,

Grandmother,
who gave me these wide hips,
this fast tongue,
this fire-for-a-life—

I am your piano.

Grandmother,
I remember the green Henry J.
I remember the 28 room house
on Colorado Street.
I remember the elevator shaft.
I remember Grandfather,
fast-talking, robust and fun—

My father called you a general.

Grandmother,
who toured the country,
a concert pianist,
at the turn of the century,

Grandmother,
who was the only child
of five to survive
a diphtheria epidemic,

Grandmother,
all of your children
were artists
and most of your grandchildren.

Grandmother,
you survived in a whirl
of God and song and family
until your brain blew up.

Grandmother,
I am your piano.

PATH

It is a well worn path, and although last night I felt claws gigantic and sharp grab at my ankles, pull, hard enough to wake me screaming, I find it comfortable enough most days following in the footprints left by Father's flat feet, soft-skinned as a boy, step after step, one following the next, gnarled as he grew older, toenails curling down, thick enough to leave their own impression, and alongside his steps, Mother's smaller ones, two to every one of his almost. She would have raced ahead except he was so long-legged and direct. The path bent into tragedy and pain as did the century. We bore up well enough. Our footsteps moved straight forward towards the god who eats itself, long curves, wide streets, manicured lawns, private golf courses, American cars. The path led out of childhood, through universities, into marriage, parenthood, and art. We did what was expected of us, more. I left the path so often I thought I had created a new one until I recognized the rhythm of their passage in my own walk, felt my child anguish and attack the way I did, noticed my husband grow distant as Father did, saw my sister fall into madness like Father's brother did, watched cancer come again, again, again. I have loved these people, the clatter of their walking is percussion to my own rhythm, the din shockingly regular, repeats itself, repeats itself, repeats. My own steps, childhood rhythm, seems to me now like melody and I'm directing traffic I'd reroute if I knew how to do it. *Oedipus old and blind. Wing footed Mercury. Diana, the huntress. Obsidian's a dark black stone, with grains of gold inside it. My child's laughter is more precious to me than the sun, his pain more violent than death. Neptune has rings and Jupiter's a star. The man is part earth, and part volcano. Woman is a gate. Follow me out.* Follow me out. We're leaving this place. We've slipped off the path. Everything's new. Anything's possible. The gods are all groaning and Father is dead. The century is turning. The path is a journey. The journey is constant. You don't go anywhere or get anything. You become.

DERELICT

A derelict is loose in her, hovering on the edge of psychotic episode, hovering in dark recesses, parking lots, hovering behind trees, in shrubbery, a derelict is waiting to chase her into traffic. He is wearing a moustache, hard steel eyes, carnival glittering teeth. A derelict shark is swimming, hanging free in her subconscious ocean, a derelict without direction, an outlaw, outpatient, out of gas, out of energy, full of disease, full of bile, evil, rage, ignorance. It is chasing her, chasing her, cracking stupid jokes about the difference between blood and stone. A derelict who hates enough to kill, who loves enough to hate, hovers on the sidewalk side of lunacy, an idiotic man, a walking ego, frozen, impotent, a man who cannot love, a man who wants to kill her is hovering, haunting and hovering, on a country road, in an urban alley, he stands, frozen like granite rocks in sea foam. Why? Or how can she open his heart? Or how can she heal him? Or why has she drawn him so near? Any distance is unbearable. Why? Or how to stop it? Or why when she turns him out does she feel like an atomic bomb is exploding in her chest? Contamination leaks out. Derelict fallout sloughs off, bleeds out, fallout. A derelict, idiotic, impotent, malignant man who loves her and leaves desolation is wandering homeless and alone on the inroads of her spine, leering and chasing anything that sparks life, he is bolting out of caves, leaping out of water, stalking her in parking lots, chasing, stalking. How to cure it? Or calm it? How to love him? A derelict, outcast, sick, hungry and exhausted killer roams the landscape of her dreams, haggard and unloved.

TIRADE 6082

It is the middle of the afternoon. I am a woman who is being consumed by her own power. And the child is lighting matches, burning pieces of tissue paper on the bathroom floor, to watch the flames, to get even with me because I am not paying attention to him—anger at the child who has taken so much time, who is trying to burn my house down, and I am angry at a man who has left me hanging on a hook, and I am angry at myself for having hooks, and I am angry because it's hard to make a living. I am angry because I had to borrow money to refinance the house my son is trying to burn down. I would like to clear away my problems and not pass them on to the child, but I don't know how to stop being mad. I am mad at a man who raped my friend, and I am angry at the priest who burned me at the stake 400 years ago. I am angry. I am angry at myself for not being able to open my heart to love, and it grieves me and makes me furious. And I can still smell smoke in the bathroom. I am a grown woman who shakes with rage, who walks straight at whatever she attracts. I am angry at how girls were raised to wait for men, who don't know what they're doing, to make decisions. I am angry at women who are receptive and patient. I do not feel patient, I do not feel like being a good mother to a child who is trying to set the house on fire, and I do not feel like waiting for anyone to unhook me, forgive me, open or close to me. I don't know how to stop it, the rage. I don't know how to keep it from killing everything I care about. I don't know how to accept twenty centuries of oppression, that says women are property, that builds religions based on misogyny, that broke my mother's heart and her mother's heart, that pours anti-psychotic drugs into my sister, who can hardly make it through a day because the burden is so great. I am angry at myself for being too angry to forgive or give up fighting. I am a grown woman who pounds her fists against walls in order to keep from striking a child who is trying to set her house on fire.

Walk it out, run it out, dance it out, sing it out, let it go, hang it on the moon. Let it go, fight it out, never stop, dance it out, love it out, let it out in slow rolling lines. Scream it out, dance it out, let it go, that the fury may pass through, that the light may shine again, that water may clear your heart. Sweat it out, cry it out, love it out, laugh it out, play it out, let it go. Stop! giving it to the children, or they will burn the house down.

WITCH

I remember the smoke,
how cloud blue eyes held mine
to the last instant,
as I fell into darkness—
as flames climbed my spine,
death shriek,
pain beyond
endurance,
the bond held.
And when I died,
you lost the woman
in yourself.

It was Faith, or Reason,
as you oddly call it,
against Nature—me.
You were chanting,
Priest, and praying,
as flames raged around me,
you were singing
litanies about passion,
that extrapolate to fire,
blue eyes
magnetized to
green eyes,
sea and sky.

Now,
when you look at me,
and see Modern Woman,
in fact,
I am the one
you sacrificed
and there isn't a cell
in my body that can
forget terror
of fire,
or your blue eyes
melting
me to ash,

and I can only grieve
for both of us.

Three hundred years ago
and yesterday,
you came looking for a cure.
We walked along the river,

> *a curative for sanguine,*
> *root for toothache,*
> *poultice for cough,*
> *tincture for headache,*
> *charm for pestilence.*

The old women gave me
this magic, taught me
the cycles
of earth and star, taught me
to bathe in moonlight,
and let pain out
with monthly blood.

> *Magic mixed with our steps.*
> *It blessed is, it blessed plants,*
> *tree roots, galaxies and sun.*

We found leeches,
ferns, berries,
and gently, slowly at first,
with halting steps,
full of surprise,
we found each other,
two bodies curled
into a holy nest,
leaf mulch,
smell of earth
reaching for fertility,

> *and of each*
> *there was no part*

that did not bless
the other.

How you turned that!
to evil
is how you died,
watching me die
for trumped up charges:

> *dancing in moonlight*
> *fornicating with frogs*
> *speaking in strange tongues,*
> *striking sheep blind*
> *flying around Venus,*
> *leaping into or out*
> *of tree limbs,*
> *cooking cat eyes*
> *or buzzard wings,*
> *for being beautiful,*
> *for growing old*
> *and wise,*
> *for loving you.*

I see today
that you want me again.

Prepare to be tested.
Know that the stakes
are high,
the fire is mine.
I am
the revolution.

The wheel
has stopped at you.
And I do not like
priests.

THE MYTHICAL MAN

has been pulling me out of my skin since I outgrew the first yellow dress Mother made. I liked it, yellow buttons, pleats, linen tie. It was the first piece of clothing I remember and I was furious when I grew out of it. *Why can't you make it bigger?* She simply said, *I can't.* Since before that the Mythical Man has been pulling my soul out of the ordinary things in life, a bowl of cereal in the morning, an infant looking up at the ceiling wondering why it is alone, hunger, born someplace in pre-conscious sludge, connected to abandonment and loss. The Mythical Man is a ghost, seductive and almost always gone. He has been calling me, writing songs to me, asking for appointments when there isn't any time, finding love in corners of me I didn't know existed, hitting center, again and again, *HA! Gotchya!* He doesn't sweat. He doesn't even breathe hard. Who wouldn't be in love with him? He must be a god. I have married him, been his lover, been his mother, and his friend. I have loved him, set him free, raised him, healed him, and given him more life than I have to make him happy and he hates me. He hates me because we hate ourselves. Our mothers taught us this with the vengeance of their own lost lives, taught us how to fight for space they never had by killing love. Sometime, a thousand years ago, or yesterday, he was jealous of me, of the balance or grace, of the creative force, but now he's won. He's better than I am at almost everything, richer, more successful, younger, older, wiser and more foolish. Inside me is a Mythical Man, a figure of my own creation, who hates me.

EULOGY FOR THE ERA

Beginning with:

*Mankind, Man-made, the Common Man, Man and his world, Neanderthal
Man, the best Man for the job, when Man invented the wheel, the Sun God,
Man's achievements, Man's basic needs, the history of Black Man in America,
one small step for Man, a giant step for Mankind. Man, like other mammals,
breast-feeds his young:*

pressman, repairman, craftsman, chairman, conductor,
railroad man, switchman—
maid

salesman, newsboy, fireman, foreman
master, policeman, watchman—
laundress

clergyman, delivery man, fisherman,
lineman, jack-of-all-trades—
wife

*We hold these truths to be self-evident: That all men are created equal—the
farmer and his wife, the lawyer and his child, the poet and his wife, the teacher
and her class.*

*The Greeks mistreated their wives. Columbus discovered America. The settlers
moved west with their wives and their cattle. A man makes art because he has
to, Doctor Jones and his pert wife Jane. Marie Curie, the beautiful chemist,
Elinor Wylie, the fiery redhead, Amy Lowell,
the queer duck!*

Masculine: resembling man, having vigor and strength.
Feminine: resembling woman, showing delicacy and weakness.

*I'll have my girl make your reservations. Union members and their wives are
invited. You drive like an old woman. The ladies chatted about the draft. Sally's
husband lets her work part-time. Children look to their fathers for strength and
courage. In the delicate recesses of the female mind is the seed of love.*

We look to:

wise men to free us from superstition and from the *old wive's tales* of our *forefathers*. The litany repeats. Words and the people they create move in pilgrimage across the earth, a woman, whose spine is a footprint.

WILL

I don't know what to do with my body. I really don't.
I wouldn't mind being buried the old way, except where?
My parents have chosen to be cremated, vials stored in California,
have abandoned the graveyard at Four Corners
where five generations of the family are entombed,
Father never liked *the old longbeards* anyhow.

And I don't like the idea of being burned, remember too much
about witches, the shadow and smoke lurk in my history.
Fire doesn't appeal to me, but then—
once you're dead, you're gone.
Dead, *not* anymore.
Not.
So it doesn't matter.
In theory.

Perhaps I could be made into a component of paper,
ashes turned to pulp, then made into a special edition
of my last work, called **Special Edition.**
I could be a limited edition.
They could print until the cells ran out.
I could be collected someplace people have to get special
permission to get into, or chained to a thick oak table,
or set under glass, gilded, watercolored, lacquered.

Maybe in a hundred years the **Special Edition** could be burned
and scattered in space, or maybe
just archived in a star ship library where memory chips
are litanies of poetry, or chocolate, or music.

I don't know what to do with my body. I really don't.
Perhaps it could be made into a glaze and put on plates.
In my will it could say:
These are to remain in the family forever.

I'd like my ashes to be spread over Barton Springs, at dawn,
 on Winter Solstice, but I wouldn't like it if someone else
did that to the water I swim in every day.

I don't know what to do with my body. I really don't.
I work all the time. There are bills and debts, phone calls
and commitments. I'm usually behind and can't get all
the work done, and the child is demanding
and there are people I care about who take time.
I don't have much time to think about myself.

I remember a time, fifteen years ago, or in another life,
when I was consumed with my innermost feelings,
now they seem irrelevant. Frankly,
it doesn't matter how I feel, the world is plain hostile.
I'm fine, but conditions are terrible.
And the first day in ten months I have time
to think about myself, here I am writing a will,
and wondering what to do with my dead body.

Maybe,
I'll donate it to the nuclear accelerator at Stanford.
I remember driving along it for a long time,
California foothills rising in the distance,
fog rolling, golden long-grass bending to the wind.

I tried to imagine a microscopic particle traveling as fast
as it is possible to go in order to run head-on into another particle
traveling as fast as it is possible to go in the opposite direction.
The idea pleased me.

How many particles are there in a human body?
How many collisions am I capable of?
I don't know what to do with my body. I really don't.

WHITE PAINT AND BLUE TRIM

Blue trim and white paint.
White paint,
White paint.
White paint and blue trim.
It is summer in Texas,
and I am painting the outside
of my house with a brush.
Blue trim, blue trim,
window sash, roof eves.
White paint and blue trim.

I am compelled to cover
all visible surface area
with white paint and blue trim.
I cover myself.
White arms and blue armpits.
White legs and blue kneecaps.

The banker who just substituted
a three-year balloon for a
fifteen-year note would look good
with a blue mouth and white hair,
a blue asshole and white feet.

White paint and blue trim.
My brush reaches for the sky;
the colors match exactly.
That does not make me a painter.
I am a woman.
I am standing on a ladder.
It is 102 degrees, and the sun
has almost crossed to this side of
the house.

I do not paint this house
for myself.
I do not paint it for my children
or for the man I love.
I paint it for a banker who

will tell me in three years
to give him face value of the note
or this house,
with white paint and blue trim.

I am painting over old paint.
I am painting over rotten wood.
I am painting over broken glass and cobwebs.
I am painting over red ants and wasp nests.
My fingers stick together.

In a few months I will sell this house.
I will turn the money for the blue and white
banker into one dollar bills.
If I were one inch taller,
I could reach the top of the eve
without moving the ladder.

IN THE RETIREMENT COMMUNITY

there are no black people, or brown ones. Everyone speaks English. Children are not allowed. You cannot own property there or rent if you are under fifty, or unless you can afford housing that starts at $200,000. In this century, at this moment, that is more than a family of four below the poverty line will earn in a hundred years. There are private swimming pools, saunas, jacuzzis, golf courses, club houses, restaurants and shops. There are monitors who question strangers, demanding to see visitor passes. Visitors have to follow rules. When I visit I swim in an outdoor pool so hot it makes me sweat. In winter steam blocks the sun. I think about how much these people have, how greedy they have been, how they have used up the earth, how they sacrificed their sons to a war in Vietnam with no reason behind it, knee jerk patriotism they have too much invested in to evaluate. I think about oil spills and homeless people. I think about the national debt. I think about interest rates. I think about how their children can never be as prosperous as they have been because the world economy is staggering under the weight of a debt they increased in geometric progressions. I think of how they have lived, thoughtless of the earth. I think of the way the generation that saved the world for democracy ate it up, poisoned it, bought it, sold it, lied to it, stole it, hid it, enslaved it, burned it and now owns every square foot of it. And I want to know why this pool is private and why these people are rude and abrasive even to their own children. When I swim in their private pool, I see hands reaching out for everything, grabbing. I think about blindfolds. I see people who have squeezed the last juice out of life and are waiting to die. I see terror rise in them. I see the last generation of prosperous Americans.

MOTHER'S VISIT

Mother's visit was horrendous. There wasn't an instant when she wasn't angry about something someone was doing or had done. The child was sick so she banned him from the kitchen and guest room. She scrubbed everything with bleach, wore herself out scrubbing, had no energy for anything else. Trips were out, we were locked in a tight knot of contagion. In the bathroom our toothbrush holder was horrifying to her, the kitchen cabinets were filthy. The moment she walked in the guest room a large cockroach walked across the floor. She thought it was a mouse. She found ants and moths in the cabinets. The dog slept under her bed and she was bitten by a flea. I was given food and medicine lists every morning, spent hours buying potions and bland food. It took us too long to put the chicken away. She said that chicken was dangerous, that it would spoil and make her sick. She said the refrigerator was broken, the cabinet mirror was too foggy for her to see herself in, the man should get another job, he came home too late and left too early. He hadn't finished fixing up the house. She said where she lived people weren't allowed to leave trash cans in the front yard. She wanted me to call the doctor twice a day to be sure she wouldn't catch the child's flu. I spent $65 finding out he didn't have strep which wasn't surprising since he didn't have a sore throat. She didn't want to attend a party for my business, smiled uncomfortably when I mentioned it until I understood she didn't want to risk looking at who I have become, would rather cringe at my poor housekeeping, at contagion, would rather complain about the unfinished remodel job than enjoy our new house, rather cringe at insects than acknowledge a pesticide-free environment. I tell myself over and over again *She is your mother. Do not get angry at your mother.* Sometimes when I'm about to shout her down, I see Father's spirit lurking in the shrubbery, scowling at me. He taught us to humor her. He said she was incapable of understanding that she hurt us and there wasn't any point in making her miserable. He loved her. Years of anger flows back to the self, depression blooms in our hearts, a universe of self-incrimination. When my son gets furious at his grandmother, I don't tell him to humor her. I say, *Let it rip!*

AMERICAN FAMILY, GENERIC

The child has been having problems. He is negative about everything, sure things won't work out, sure he can't accomplish new work, sure his life will fall into chaos, sure he won't have any friends at school, sure he won't be able to have this or that, sure he will do his work incorrectly, sure he won't be a good soccer player, sure that his mother is mad at him. She is not angry at him. She is negative. There is too much debt and not enough money. Her father died. She has blown up and doesn't look like herself, can't carry all the burdens that have found her, can't find enough hours in the day, is trying to be Superwoman, is not sure what she wants, is broken far beneath the shield, is weak and unsure and under attack from people who can't reach her when she's strong. Her mother says these problems will go away if she gives up art. Her mother offers advice, but not solace, lost in her own grief, how can she help? Her mother says she needs insurance and a retirement plan. The husband says summer is coming. He wants to go fishing. They can't afford medical insurance, or time off. There is barely enough time to sleep. The husband says she has a rotten attitude, says he hates the way his life is full of labor that is meaningless. The generation that used up the earth wants to spend money. Why aren't the children more gracious? Why isn't the house fixed? Why don't they wear better clothes? Why is it so hot? Why do bill collectors call? The generation that used up the earth calls it, *Bad Management*, asks, *Why don't you save money so you'll have some when you run out?* They elect politicians who pretend to balance a national debt they sowed like bad seed.

ERRORS

He is ashamed of errors. They don't make him want to improve. They make him want to hide. The teacher doesn't have time for conferences; he is too busy finding errors. Last month the child drew a picture of a cute little boy, smiling, wearing a gigantic hat and walking shorts with fun designs on them. He wrote a word on the shirt. It was spelled wrong. I corrected it. He took back the drawing and covered the boy's face with scar/scribble marks. I said he had just showed me it hurt his feelings to make mistakes. We put the picture on the wall to help us remember how sensitive a child is about mistakes. Errors. I am a teacher. I find errors in people's writing. Editors find errors in mine. The ones I just made will cost $300 and six days to fix, six days this month will cost a thousand dollars in December. Once I made a mistake that cost eleven years. Some mistakes are too close to speak of. We all make them. And we hate them. And they make our faces fierce with scar/scribble marks. Sometimes we try to cover them up, hide them. Sometimes we are so ashamed we don't speak of them. Sometimes we bury our heads in the sand and pretend we don't have backsides. Sometimes picking on somebody else—another country, a child, a parent—dulls the aggravation. *X—work harder. X—this is not right. X—you must not have been listening to me. X—you are trying to hide your mistakes. X—you were playing the piano in music class. X—you weren't listening to the teacher. X—you didn't memorize answers for the test. X—you were thinking of your own answers. I do my work and he just puts X,* the child tells me. A boy and his mother, on a brilliant autumn day, looking for a way to make peace with errors.

SUICIDE

There are ways to quit living.

You can absorb someone else,
live their life.
You can fill your time up
with crises so that
life is something
that happens to you,
you don't have to initiate.

You can hold your breath,
or drown
in tears that won't stop
falling out of your head,
out of the pit of your stomach,
tears that pull out pieces
of tissue,
scraps of muscle,
tears that leave you
exhausted.
You can drown in that.

I used to like to imagine
driving off a bridge,
or into a highway embankment.
I like to think about
drawing a sharp razor blade
across my wrists, up my arms.

A good way to quit living
is to take on more responsibility
than you can be responsible for,
go into debt,
like the world has,
then gamble with the debt
and lose.

I understand why people
jumped out of windows
during the Great Depression,

or why people turn on gas jets
and go to sleep.

You can take pills.
There are all kinds of ways
to stop living.
You can refuse to solve problems.
You can stay someplace after
your time there is over.
You can refuse to open your heart.
You can stop living
by accident or out of stupidity.
You can step in front of a
moving train,
cross the street at the wrong
instant,
catch a stray bullet,
join the army
or fuck until you don't exist.

You can
sacrifice
every instant
to the needs
of a child,
or a partner,
or parent,
a cat, a hamster,
or a career.
You can kill yourself
with guilt,
fear or hate.
Some people use guns.
Some people create wars.
Some people turn themselves inside out
every fourth year so that
eventually what kills them
is exposure.

There are all kinds of ways
to die and you don't have to be
dead to enjoy them.

THE HOLE IN 22ND STREET

I watched them dig. With exquisite tenacity they sank it down through vast white limestone, chunks blowing up sky high, and still they kept on blasting, a great hole. With barricades to keep us out. And so when I drive up 22nd Street, I go long way around. That's what I've learned. I've learned to go the long way around the hole at the end of 22nd Street. I don't care how good it looks, with bridges, traffic, ambulance, police car, underpass, overpass. I know a hole when I see one. It is an expensive hole, cranes the height of a city block, work crews with hard hats and hungry children, explosives, earth moving machines, block and tackle work, seismographic records of the earth ripped open. I say someone went to a lot of trouble to dig that hole. I say it's there. Do not phase out listening to the radio and let signs lure you to the center of it, wide green state highway signs that say: **Capitol, 6th Street, Downtown,** signs saying: **University, Cultural Events.** Do not look down and see a galaxy explode, or someone crying half a lifetime, pulling out eyelashes, directing traffic around an idiot automobile they let break down, do not see vacant hollow eyes boring into your heart, mumbling lips spilling stupid sexist idiot talk from pockets, draining intellect, blowing bubbles, do not see the old man shake head back and forth: *At the center of every heart is a vast pool of insanity. Your grandmother for instance was a missionary. After the fourth child died in one week from diphtheria, she woke up on Sunday morning and went out to praise the Lord, long black veils trailing behind her.* Who knows how much it cost, the hole in 22nd Street.

A blue hearse full of surprises speeds down grey slick pavement. A man slips out, scans my body, mind and life, inside, out, says *Big Deal*, and moves to Cleveland. A tall man whose long legs and hard eyes fit exactly the space inside for grief wrings out endless crying, oceans of pouring out grief, flood gates open and shut like lies. Grief, for children who are dead, for a clown whose daughter found him hanged by the neck on the back porch one morning before daylight, face grey, contorted with pain, with wide-eyed questioning grief, turned into a crackling fire of jokes spilled out over the desert, ashes rolling into tumble weeds, random and irrelevant blowing against fences that are the limits of understanding. It is grieving for the living, the pull into sorrow, it is grieving for the dead, long gone and recent, it is the instant snap of flesh breaking through a pane of window glass, jagged edges diving into fingers and palm, the swift flow of blood after that. Ritual chunks of flesh drop off, retribution. It is a great wave of anger played out in burlesque studios, under light, with dialogue: *He is my husband.* (enter children) *You are a mistake.* It is a long swell of rage curved back at self, the danger of that steeping like a wrong herbal tea, bounding up, leaping with primal energy to high spirit, or joke, to magnet, or killing. *Why did you kill him then? I didn't like his shirt.* It is that and more of course, the signs that lead into the hole at the end of 22nd Street, arrows, white letters on green background, clean and clear indications: **Turn Here, One Way,** you might as well go straight to the hospital down the street and check into the mental ward. It's worth it to spend a few extra minutes, to go long way round, long way around the hole at the end of 22nd Street.

A concave slab of junk vibrates like plant food but there are no flowers, no roses called *Queen Elizabeth, Pascalli, Peace.* It is a way of drowning in small things like missing the bus every day for two years. It is the kind of insecurity that makes you count the eggs in a carton to be sure there's a dozen, that sends you back to the market five times to get garlic salt. It digs around in the past, in your work, in your garden, nothing is left unchallenged, everything is judged, then discarded. It does not recede like flood water, it carries an eternal basket of props, brass washers, gold net, finger clamps, vices, old mannequins, puppets, cactus, doll houses, spotlights. It is an allegorical play about a child dying of cancer, how you travel across the country, crawl in under his skin, pull malignant tumors off the bones, out of tissue, out from under muscle, how he dies then. It is fresh air and rain juxtaposed against the gold-toothed maniac in the blue hearse who drives back and forth over your heart. It is you rising up like Judith who came into the tent of the conquering general with wine and succulent food, fed him, then posted his head on the gate as she left. It is about how after that she went back to a quiet life of sewing, lived alone, never went outside again. It is about anger and the internalization of every aspect of experience so that the universe recreates itself inside one heart and ceases to exist out-of-doors where real trees sway in breezes that come up from the Gulf of Mexico and down from the Arctic Sea. It is an internal cycle of patterned strife, waves of oppression, grief.

Click: Loud wheels of the hearse click behind you, hurl a fist of insults at your face, a vehicle full of aliens beam death out of their antlers, scan the street with search lights: bottle caps, street lights, traffic signals, fire engines, winos, an ambulance, street fights, hookers, music blaring out of late night bars, pickup trucks, cowboys, paper blowing across an intersection. *Click*: Dollars and coins fly through the air like radar. *Click*: Distortions curve asphalt back on itself. You send messages out, they spiral to zero. You end up in Brazil or Guatemala where there are no words for what you set down when you left home the first time: the blue hearse, the driver, a sack full of wind, the devil, the shrew, a set of false teeth. An old man in Columbia made up by Marquez, chained to an oak tree says: *Right there across the river are all kinds of magical instruments while we go on living like donkeys.* But in fact, the only thing over there is a big hole. A hole full of bad ideas like Christianity, that kill you in ritual violence each afternoon at five p.m., slash veins, feel around for the soul, eat it, slosh through the arteries to the heart, drink it, ideas that start with suffering then suck you into a knot and hurl you down sputtering like a duck into nothing, into a hole, a linear map of your life rolled up and pressed to zero, zero struggle and accomplishment. The boundaries you have crossed, inconsequential. It's worth it to spend a few extra minutes. That's what I've learned. I have learned to go the long way around the shrieking and spiraling, long way around the sirens and police cars, long way around the iron-fisted daemon scratching woman fighting, but spiraling into the hole, the hole at the end of 22nd Street.

HISTORY AND SEX

I want it all—one of those stupid things she says because she refuses to edit her life. He said, *There are so many emotions.* She said, *How I feel is every way there is to feel.* They spin, reel, shock and blast out, float free-style between Venus and Orion. *What is going on?* Confusion blurs, they coast. The more she shields the stronger he breaks through. She opens; he slams shut. The pieces of his life vibrate, rattle. Impatient and stubborn, she works out of traps, asks him to drop the contest. He can't. She is threatened by his chaotic behavior but he returns full of light. She is cautious. Then he's gone. Even though he's here, he's gone, leaves saying she doesn't exist. Exist! Does not exist! She gives up, and the voice that sends her away is the voice of 4000 years of patriarchal rule, is the voice of priests who killed women for being wise, is the voice of kings and fathers who put women in angel costumes or scarlet clothing and never connected passion to soul, is the voice of men who have owned women. He doesn't hear that in his voice because he does not understand history. She quits and the force that sends her away is a voice that says *woman is 'other', exists for self, self is man.* It is a cold voice, impervious and full of chaos. He does not like that part of his voice and has no idea where it comes from. She points. *Here it is! This is the problem. This is why we hurt each other. Here. Look at it.* There is a long silence. Mind opens, then slams shut. *Can you be a little nicer?* she asks. But he does not know how.

BECAUSE OF RAPE

for Susan Lee

I have watched you stretch to reflect violence that is not a reflection of your mythic reality, not your hidden dreamscape. Who has not dreamed of being hunted, caught, or raped? You did nothing to attract attack! Were at home sleeping in your bed, awakened to worse than nightmare—**Evil,** not the idea of evil, but the thing itself, **Evil**—a static, untransformable mass, violent and incapable of redemption. *Feed, feed the creative force in your heart, body, mind. There is no other answer.* And the new husband, gone within weeks of the attack, chose your instant of greatest need to leave. We could not save you from the dark tunnel, could not save you from the water dance that almost killed you, lost and naked in the Ozark mountains for two nights, and you saying, *I would have traded every man I've ever known for a thermal blanket.* You, last week, saying you were going to find the rapist, give him an award for doing the least amount of harm to you a man ever has! He didn't tie you to a bad marriage for twenty-one years, he didn't abandon you and two small babies, or open your heart with fast passion, and then abandon it. *The rapist only hurt for fifteen minutes!* Dark humor, pain, asleep in your bed, terror and violent hatred of woman. Stench of **Evil**. And since then you have been traveling and your passage has left them all behind. *Your light in the hearts of the ones you love is clear, is healing, it has always been so, now you are stronger than you used to need to be, light flares!*

        No one evolves
         on purpose.

You on a plateau
where
water pours life force
from the center
of woman indomitable—

        deep oracle
        carved out of
        pain,
        open—
        like any waterfall.

Let the song unfold.
Let the song unfold,
sing to us,
woman of pain
and power,
sing to us,
the song of rebirth,
the song of woman
alone on the mountain,
naked, cold, lost,
sing to us the song
of a million women
violated,
let the tone be harsh
and let is pass
through all of us
until it echoes
until it reverberates
against the walls
of history
where it is etched
in stone:
women are chattel,
women are evil,
women are property,
woman was made
from Adam's rib,
women are spoils
of war,
women are witches,
women are nags,
women are to be
taken,
let the walls
of history
vibrate! fall
of their own weight.

707 DELTA JET AIRLINER

Something fell
out of the hatch
of
a 707 Delta
jet airliner
flying
from San Francisco
to Salt Lake City,
Salt Lake City
to San Antonio,
from San Antonio
to Mexico City.

It was a suitcase
full of clothing
she needed
to lose—
a man's blue striped
shirt,
with a man in it,
posturing
out of fear,
fearing
out of pain,
waving
his arms
at her
from below
on the desert
outside
Phoenix.

Sadder than
that,
out fell
her sister,
mother,
father,
his mother,

his father,
all the fathers
and
children,
thousands of them—
a trail of life
in the ionosphere.

They all
fell out
of a suitcase
that was
dumped
for no reason
out of the hold
of a 707 Delta
jet airliner
flying
across America
last Wednesday
evening.

They fell
out
when
she stopped
holding
on.

MENSTRUAL HUT

Mine is urban, a dark room, heat. I crave heat to sweat out poison, anger, pain. I require a full moon, nerves entwined in moonlight, I hold off pain until she rises, round and salmon, rust on the horizon, then drain out another cycle. I require candlelight and moonlight, incense and a hot bath, steaming so it almost blisters, oil. I gather shelter, fall into pain, headache, cramping, a dark hole. I stop eating meat, ingest calcium and iron, chew on cornstarch, bloat and swell up. In daylight I squint. Sometimes energy flows out of me so fast I can't hang on to anything, spill coffee, end relationships, drop images into the void; sometimes I am droll, exhausted for three days, tired past the help of sleep. Always I mourn life force pouring out of me, through me; always I am inconsolable and dark. Sometimes when chunks of blood pass out I'm frightened, remember embryo bleeding out, flood of red, hemorrhage, how close I've been to death: life/death, woman/body, cyclic wax and wane, human pain, death of women in childbirth, insides pouring out. Out. I stretch to touch the pain, then let it go. I go into the menstrual hut to recover, I go into the menstrual hut because I can't avoid it, I go into the menstrual hut because I hurt, deep inside, woman place, fiber tearing apart. It is an urban hut made out of sheet rock and stone tile. It is a place where men can't reach me. I am invisible except for grass and bamboo reflected in the green of my eyes, invisible except for smoke pouring out skin vents or the cloud that settles on my gloss as if I were mourning. And I am. When I was young we didn't speak of it. I don't even remember when I first *got* the *curse*, as if something external came to *punish* me. I had to grow into the menstrual hut, long wrenching years of self creation that peeled off layer and layer and layer of malevolence until I found me here, walking a moonpath that leads in cycles to the menstrual hut, ancient intersection where blood hits the external world and woman exists.

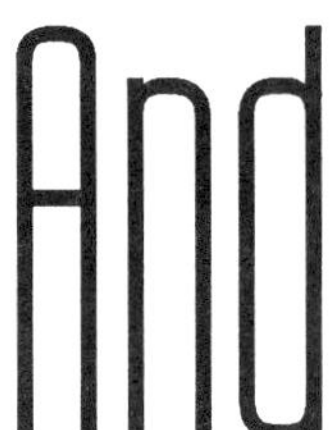
And

THE WAYFARER

The wayfarer,
Perceiving the pathway to truth,
was struck with astonishment.
It was thickly grown with weeds.
Ha, he said,
I see that no one has passed here
In a long time.
Later he saw that each weed
was a singular knife.
Well, he mumbled at last,
Doubtless there are other roads.

Stephen Crane

ICE

In 22-degree-below-zero weather, just after midnight, the family station wagon slipped off a Minnesota farm road and stalled. Numb limbs of roadside trees cut up to a blue indigo knife cold sky, stars brilliant, as close as her crystalline breath, she wrapped a cloth coat close to her body, pulled on knit mittens, straightened her cap and began to walk, the heels of her leather boots made a hollow sound on the ground as she walked, would walk two miles, her only choice. Walking into numbness, she thought of Wally, Wally down the road, he would be home, she would call her parents from there, they would laugh at the close call and say, *You could have frozen to death out there. No more going out after midnight for you in the winter.* They would bring the pickup to get her, would be angry, but glad to see her alive. She would walk. The sky, metallic, a flat moon ringed with two crystal halos moved more and more slowly along with her as she walked. Finger tips, toes, cheeks, nose, were numb and wildly separate from her simple rhythmic motion. The craters of the moon were as close and distant as Highway 2, four miles down the road. Each turn of the road, the bent tree stump there, on the other side a small pond, the hole in the fence here, a clump of trees, the curve where deer cross, every part of the road she took comfort from lifelong knowledge of, as familiar to her as the family cat, but as she walked it shifted direction, seemed to slip back toward the Indian reservation, White Earth Reservation, so true a name you never thought about it, white earth, across it she walked, alongside the road, nothing moved as down silver hillside—*skate blades glinting starlight in long elegant glide, silver blonde hair slick as glacier melt, emerald green eyes, gloves of white leather, soft white leather scarf, gliding smoothly down graves, the Ice King spun to a stop beside her, took her hand. They danced across a vast white field to mirrored rainbow sound strung of starlight. She gazed into his eyes, his held her attention, hypnotic, as if their deep emerald light could rivet her soul to the earth as she walked. They danced, gliding to peaks of the great white mountains of Alaska, and down they spun, faster than light, down velvet snow of glacier, down ice water beams that refracted infinite energy in delicate crystalline patterns. Mandalas grew even in her heart as she walked, powder blew up around her heels. She moved with exaggerated weight in slow motion inside the crystal circles of the moon. His laughter was a fleece chord, high pitched. He told her of a magnificent ice palace underground, he would take her. She would melt into it as if through shattered glass, could look back at earth from far away as they made fine delicate love, cool moonlight fell on taut skin as they slipped through each other, etching thin lines of future, the pitch nearly un-*

bearable. Coming out of his house the next morning, Wally found her, stiff as a board, fifteen feet from his front door. Her face was ashen. He picked her up like a piece of lumber, put her slantwise in the back of his truck and drove through the thin morning air to the hospital in Fosston, to a doctor who said: *She's frozen solid, like a piece of meat taken out of the deep freeze. I can't get a hypodermic into her. Her eyes are like green glass and register no light. There is no pulse.* The reaction began three hours after she started to melt. Wrapped in water-type heating bags, she received oxygen. Hospital staff heard little whimpers, probably air coming out of her lungs. She took breaths two or three times a minute. *I can't explain why she's alive,* the doctor said. The woman herself said afterwards, *At worst I might lose a couple of toes. If I thought he'd come back, I might do it again.*

EDGE

a place where land drops off
above, for instance,
water, silver moonlight
on emerald rippling surface—

They hang on to each other, to the edge, to lush vegetation, rough granite, and below them, the abyss, space, unbearable darkness of nothing, of failure. Juniper, pine cones, maiden hair fern, delicate water fall, wet smelling earth: *It's straight down sweetheart*, he says. They hang on to each other, touching special places, nerve centers, until they're lost someplace solid, an ancestral bed, land at the center of the continent instead of here, on the edge, where they could crash at any instant. *How'd you like to drop 3000 feet?* She says she is indomitable, maybe so, but chances are there's going to be a crash: the whole bit, furniture, dishes, car payment, appliances, books, paper flying everyplace, dust devils in the wind. And they escape into love making, eyes closed to the dragon beneath the cliff, magic to help them soar, satin wings, skin stretched far enough that hard rock and falling appear feathered—the river below the cliff holds. Silver water in moonlight turns into nickels and pennies, ripples turn into dollar bills and arms reaching for them. There are not enough dollar bills. There are too many arms. They are naked, arms and body hair, legs and toes, necks and bellies raked by arctic winds. They are hanging on to the edge.

DON'T STAND IN FRONT OF A MOVING TRAIN

is a rule I invented in the sixties,
when America was like an old time movie,
a train barreling down,
ragtime piano and suspense,
a heroine tied to the railroad track,
and it seemed like, unless
you were hog-tied, a sensible
person would get out of the way.

I invented it shortly before
I got fired
for giving radical material
to high school students.
So I altered it
(because you never know
when they're going to get you) to:
Don't stand in front
of the same moving train
twice.

I carried the rule with me
when I moved to Texas,
but didn't see the train coming
until I was flat on my back.
So I altered it again:
Try to recognize
a moving train
when it's running over you,
which should have done the trick
except I shared it with a man
who said it was
good art.

Just words on a video screen:
DON'T STAND
IN FRONT
OF A MOVING TRAIN,
then a locomotive coming at you.

DREAMING THE FAMILY

The instruments you had invented were like jet engines, turbo devices no one could play, but a crazy country jig came out anyway and the people loved it. You were trying to sing, but words came out bent. You whispered something to me, a woman struggling to stay awake in the front row, worn to exhaustion, caught in a net of being, thread of spirit, thread of endurance, thread of light. You said later we'd go out. I said I was already out. I said you were warm. And you were. I had been walking in the rain and was cold, cold and exhausted. Your heat radiated into me, you said your family was here. I miss the musicians who filled my family with melody, musical rigmarole, notes and scales, laughter and melody, melody—glistening like diamonds, melody—before the family was blasted apart. The music stayed in the mountains, in Pennsylvania and UpperNewYorkState. That's what they call it, to distinguish it perhaps from the City, NewYorkCity—it wasn't that kind of music. It was violin concertos, piano sonatas, flute exercises and church music, dancing was forbidden—but campsongs were all right, the funnier the better. The ones who stayed kept the music. The ones who left were artists and writers. Maybe it wasn't the American migration that fragmented my family. Or grief. What if it was aesthetic differences? Or diction? I have a habit of loving people who are distant, singing people full of melody and joks, distant, full of rigmarole. And the love comes back to me in a long serenade, always has, the singers long gone. *Family, broken and fragmented American family, family, soul/family of those who have been one since the first cell split apart in sea water, family, a child with a sore throat, or cancer, family, passionate oneness with the universe, a song, a catalyst, someone distant and familiar, someone tangled in bedsheets.* What is woman but an artist making images of the chaotic heart of the family? You mirror me back to myself, I who am usually lost, find me, reflected in diamond rigmarole, I laugh, or cry, my heart opens, is warmed at the heat of your fire, a fire I can see from a distance, spirits entwined, without feet, we move fast, you and I, drunk on a passionate feast of art, *family. Family fragmented and transformed, the family you are born with and the one your heart flies to, family. Family.*

POST OFFICE

I get mail,
a lot of it.
And I don't always answer it,
or open it,
or read it.
This morning on the telephone
I found out
a certified letter
I had ignored
contained a cashier's check
for $1000.
I'd been wondering how I would
make all the things
happen this month
that needed to occur
without another $1000.
I'd been worrying.
I'd been scrambling to scrape up pieces
of a thousand dollars.
The scraps fell short.
I was floating on chance, floating checks,
riding on stress, living the American way.
But it was unnecessary.
What I needed was at the post office.
And when I picked up my mail—

It was you,
stepping out of a long serenade,
to continue a conversation begun when I was
asleep.

AGAIN THE TRAIN

For many years I warned myself
not to, but did it anyway, I stood in front of moving trains.
It was a compulsion.

A friend
who is smarter than I, told me to get
a moving cart.

I wasn't convinced.
I tried to stay away from moving trains, shut the rhythm
out of my heart.

It reminded me
of tornadoes, it reminded me of the man I saw get run over
by a train.

And still I dream
of trains, long shining slick and black shafts of energy
tunneling,

tunneling
into the unknown, going someplace fast, someplace vast
and terrifying.

It is a way of being trapped
and lost at the same time. It is me traveling into something
I am afraid of.

But today
I agreed to find a context in my life for the train.
I agreed

because
I have to. I agreed because I can't know where I'm going
if I refuse to go.

About trains,
you don't stand if front of them,
you ride.

FLASHBACK

Party hats and margueritas, streamers, chocolate, lovers, brothers, rows of every kind of pie and cake appear attached to fingers reaching out, but I hurt too much to eat cake. A man says, *It's a birthday party. It doesn't matter what you want.* The Budweiser draft team races past and I nod across to where my grandmother's horsehair chair sits empty as a church. Another slice falls out: *brother is gone. We are unbearably empty and sad. They are serving cake and I am wearing a party hat. There are steamers and clowns,* one of a thousand instants pushed back into darkness. So for years when I looked inside, there was nothing much: some photography, a yellow dress, braided hair, a brick wall. When it comes back, on the sleeve of some kind of pain, I cry, even when they are swinging at the piñata, even while I am telling jokes, to hold off the force, the adult cries tears denied the child. Somewhere in the city a siren becomes a locomotive belching steam, wheels clicking. I am mesmerized, a child standing at the end of a tunnel that is suddenly a blaze of light.

MANY-HEADED LION

You can't summon
or avoid
her,
you can't interrupt
her
or absorb her—
she is energy
attracted to light,
she rides
she rides
the many-headed lion,
and six faces shriek,
I want every atom
of experience,
and the many-headed lion
gets what
it wants.

    Red, orange, yellow
    flame! flame!
    flames leap out—
    horizons of sunrises
    spiral from the core
    of being,
    she rides
    she rides the many-headed lion
    to exhaustion,
    long, hard, full well
    she rides—
    fire woman.
    Fire!

        Body/soul soaring
        enchanted, entangled
        consumed
        consuming
        spiral out, circle back
        veer to chaos, and
        beyond that,
        song.

The awakening,
wild-eyed
disoriented
beads of sweat
float on fire
like drops of moonlight
knees weak
fly
dance,
firelight
* hot red flaring sun.*

And the woman
who rides the many-headed lion
is alive
and the lion's quiet,
fire of body-soul
quenched.

And he's not careless
of result,
the many-headed lion,
but he's a hunter
and so is she.

Jungle call,
song deeper than
bone,
and the woman
who rides the many-headed
lion,
rides past
convention,
and the woman
who rides the many-headed
lion,
rides
an ancient line
of matriarchal fire,
rides

the many-headed lion
even though it would be easier
not to,
easier
to go grocery shopping
make quilts,
polish brass,
shuffle paper,
take out the trash.

But she rides
and riding gathers
strength.

SEVENTH STREET BRIDGE

So now, we're standing up
beneath the train, or rather
underneath a bridge,
the Seventh Street Bridge.

The light
is above and to the left of us,
below and to the left of a train
overhead, and except for gravity
which never forgets what to do,
it looks as if we're safe—
except
for those guys with the knives,
over there on the right,
not to mention
our own faults.

Like pilgrims
with neon feet, we move gingerly,
circle back, off track, on track, off track
circle back.

There were supposed to be signs.
The last one was late.
We are gentle, polite,
even meek, as we beckon
the street.

MARRIAGE POEM

We begin a journey.
    We begin a journey.

We go along together.
    We go along together.

I honor your changes
    I honor your changes
and the pleasure
    and the pleasure
of your company,
    of your company,
nor contain your horizon.
    nor contain your horizon.

We go along together
    We go along together
down a line of accord
    down a line of accord
that bends around error
    that bends around error
and the unknown.
    and the unknown.

The fire of your power
    The fire of your power
shall replenish my spirit
    shall replenish my spirit
and your tears
    and your tears
shall wash clear the land
    shall wash clear the land
we travel through.
    we travel through.

I love you.
    I love you.

SUMMER SOLSTICE

In a hot
imbalance
he longs
for shelter
love
an hour
someplace dark
and
quiet,
less than that,
to see her:
great
luxury,
great wealth.

In a hot
imbalance,
communication
stifles.

He sets small goals,
to propel him
through the hour.

Dry blades of grass
like knives,
cut out yellow light.

He asks
for forgetfulness
sleep,

to fall away, to drop into
a healing
place.

He asks
for small things.
In a

hot imbalance,
a woman
bends to yellow light,

radiant,
the kind of light
that distorts space.

ART IS A LOVER WHO CANNOT STOP SINGING,

singing after midnight,
howling,
while I am asleep,

music,
like a landslide,
or waterfall,

gravel,
eloquence and melody,
standard brand cars,
something
about America—

braying
braying for love,
cowboys
on a starship,
rodeos and motel rooms.

Somehow
strains of this music
never
stop,
an obstinate
kind of hope.

Of course
the actual woman
is September sunlight
behind blue curtains,
stretched
between family
and work,
is not listening
regardless
of the fact

that the music
etches her image
in neon.

Miracles and facts.

She is dull,
cannot read jokes,
close as breath.

Distant,
as nightfall
from daylight,
time zones clash.

Here,
in the sun,
she bakes hard.
Look,
her brain nearly
explodes.

After
midnight, when she
falls to silence,
it's his turn to howl.

BOTH

Can a woman born in the flat center of America, born at the end of WWII, child of the baby boom, child of the Presbyterian Church, child of *sex is the most wonderful thing in the world*, child of *cross your legs when you sit*, child of *don't let people know how smart you are, the boys won't like it*, child of *feet and the ground are dirty*, child of *wash your hands*, and *don't touch yourself down there*, child of *good girls wait until they're married*, can a woman raised like that love two men at the same time, if they are both good men, intelligent, proud and hard working, magic and exciting, if one is her mate and the other her lover, can she love them both, a girl child from the center of America? What if she is also a child of the Sixties, of the Women's Movement, a hippie, a child of the Free Sex Movement, an artist, an attorney, a senator, an electrician, a golf pro, an iconoclast? Can she hold two men in her heart at the same time, is she free enough, can she love both men and not ask one to wear the other's hands, not attack one in order to make way for the other, can she love both? Can the men allow it or will there be a fight, a sacrifice? Can she hold two men in her heart, in her body? Is it dishonesty or fact? Can mature love and new love, its flowering hysteria, exist in the same person at the same time? Will the new man think he's stealing, does he think her life is false? Can he accept love in transition, as it falls out of a full life, can he fit it into his being, a woman stretched to fullness, past that, can he honor the miracle and manage whatever outcome evolves from it? Can the partner release hold, give space? Can any of them live with freedom? Can a woman born in the Corn Belt, the Bible Belt, the heartland of America manage any of this at all? And if not, which relationship has to be sacrificed? What does she do when the children attack, and they will, with power that's incredible. How quickly desire melts. How fast love turns to dust, how quickly life turns into a river, how obvious the answer, stop loving, stop it, stop loving both.

TUNING FORK

Mother and Father
rang
true.

It was not
enough,
they taught us,
to be beautiful.

You have to ring
clear,
sound—
like a tuning fork.

DOOR

This morning
when I took my child
to school

he didn't want to go,
tried running in with an older
boy,
who ignored him,

tried running in with a smaller
boy,
but turned at the wide tree
and came back to me.

We spoke.
He said he was afraid
of school.

I walked him
to the door. He said,
Good-bye.

I left.
One of the aides found
him running down the street

after my car,
long gone,
a little boy, sobbing

and afraid.
And yet once he got inside
he had a good time,

learned things,
talked to other
children.

The step
that goes through
a door

or across a threshold
is powerful
and terrifying.

And I
am just a child
crying in the street

outside
doors I have to make
it through

this morning
too, and
Mother drove off long ago.

AND

I grew up in
a world of
only,
live in
a world of
and.

And love for
anyone
is all the
love
you've ever known:
mother
father, sister,
brother,
son,
lover,
partner,
mate or friend.

The earliest scars
manifest
again,
again,
until we're
healed.

Of things past
healing,
there
is nothing
you can do
but change:
move,
travel,
turn into
someone else,
act,

pray,
prey,
fight
or quit.

The whirling dance
can make
you senseless.

And
no woman
ever
loves
a man
who's
not her
father, brother
lover, lovers,
or son.

And
no man
loves
a woman
who isn't
every
woman
he has
ever known.

Evidence

We tell you, tapping on our brow,
  The story as it should be,
As if the story of a house
  Were told, or ever could be;
We'll have no kindly veil between
Her visions and those we have seen,
As if we guessed what hers had been,
  Or what they are or would be.

from *Eros Tyrranos*
Edwin Arlington Robinson

MOHANDAS K. GANDHI
TWO WAY TRAFFIC AHEAD

COFFEE IN TOPEKA

She could be having his baby today,
instead they
aren't speaking.

They could be having coffee
in Topeka,
lying skin to skin
under an air conditioner
listening to music
falling in and out of sleep,
laughing
trading stories,
many stories.

They could be learning
how to sell art,
but he will not speak
to the woman
he loves.

They could be drenched
in tears,
rearranging appointments,
building apartments,
answering the mail.
They could be tangled
in African batik.

He could be free
of her,
walking out of a cycle
completed,
luxuriating in the richness
of love,
feeling good, or
at peace.

He could be honest
with himself,

reach out for companionship,
he could be lost
in the vortex
of his immobility,
of his terror,
he could be unraveling
the puzzle.

He could have honored
the woman
he loved.

He could have asked
for help
and received it.

Instead he is dead.
She could be screaming
in pain.
She could be dying
in childbirth.
They could be having coffee
in Topeka.

PUBLIC SERVICE ANNOUNCEMENT

This workshop will be
an intimidating
and scary experience
presented by an unbalanced,
irresponsible person
who will make you unhappy,
anxious and sad.

You will gain weight
and be neurotic
as a result of this
well-intentioned
but pointless journey.

Major issues
will be avoided
at all costs
unless they are depressing
and futile.

The class costs $3000
and takes ten years.

You will never be the same
again.

Reservations are necessary
as there is a long waiting list.

FAST LANE

Everybody's looking for it,
the fast lane,
where sex and fun
and money and love
and everything you ever
thought you wanted
fills up every instant
so there isn't
any down time,
freeway fantasy
eight lanes
and airplanes
coming in
for a landing
in the rear view mirror.

And the truth is
I'm full
of traffic
and your
truck's parked
sideways in
my throat,
and your
child is growing
in my body,
and your sweat
is racing through
my blood
and your hair
is caught
between my teeth
and I have to
run a business
and make a
performance
and the fast lane
is changing us,
count the cars.

They're going
everyplace,
and I got no time
to get my work
done,
more debt
than I can pay,
more passion
than I can stay
awake for,
more conflicts
than I can figure out
and if I had
time
I'd go to therapy
but I don't
so the highway
stays
with me
and I stay
driven.

And
the fast lane
is hot
and the
white light
comes
from a rage
that's four
thousand years old.

And
I can't love
enough
to forgive us
and I can't
move fast
enough

to get off
so
I am
the fast lane
and this trip
is my life.

CROWS, VULTURES, BLACK SUITS

Emerald cold water still as she enters, parts for the swimmer she is in a dream and this morning, in fact. *Onetwothree—breathe. Onetwothree—breathe*, as she turns on the fourth stroke, she can see it, emerald water, leveling white caps, air bubbles. Beyond that are crows, vultures, black suits. Her arms lap, legs scissor, breath percolates, hands cup; water drops arc, eyes shift every fourth stroke, from subterranean vision, to fast shafts of seeing that race across air. And the river moves gently, cold emerald spirals rise up from the center of the spring she swims over. They pulse like a heartbeat, heart of earth, water, emerald cold water, emerald essence of water, swirling with the turn of the planet, mercurial underneath thunder sky. She blends with the river, exhaling, inhaling, listening to the slow sound of breath under water. There's no hurry, once she's moving, cold is a part of her, hair snaps her face, wet, like snakes or a rope. She is one with the cold, is cool emerald essence. *Onetwothree—breathe, Onetwothree—breathe.* Black birds or hawks, vultures it looks like, men in black suits, silhouettes against thunder sky, ominous against thunder sky. One woman, swimming alone in the water. Above her, engineers are talking to television. *We can tear up the aquifer and not hurt it, pie charts and graphs prove it.* They are men in black suits, their beards are diplomas with no courses in literature or ethics, philosophy or art. They are standing on a hill above the cold water, making pronouncements, backs turned to the water, words pouring out. Brains light on experience, brood with theory. The swimmer calls out, *Come, stand in the water, at least turn and look at it!* Cameras click, microphones are netted against wind, thundersky rumbles disgust. *Onetwothree—breathe, onetwothree—breathe,* crow feet, beak arms, thunder mouthed babbling, death to the planet. A warning. A warning.

WHO THE HELL WAS GUSTAV?

Excuse me, a tentative voice, grey hair, sparkling eyes. I am in the parking lot of the Community College, late to teach, turn to speak. *Are you Susan Bright?* I nod. *I think you were my high school English Teacher.* Silence. *In Connecticut.* I recognize a thick Eastern accent, but am looking at a stranger. *I was in your play, Carnival. I was Gustav.* I reel back twenty, twenty-one, twenty-two years—*Carnival? What town was it?* He tells me. I am still reeling back in time. Bright eyes sparkle with mischief. *I saw your picture in the newspaper,* he says. *What are you doing here? In Texas? In the parking lot?* I ask him. It is a stupid question, as if one thinks people from the past remain constant, stick to one location. He says he teaches Physiology at the College. I'm still reeling back, boys from my classes graduating to Vietnam, was he one of them? *What year did you graduate?* For a minute he can't remember either. *1970,* my first class. Students were *engaged, engagement,* Simone De Beauvoir, the sixties, reeling back, shock after shock, the Women's Movement in New Haven, the Black Panthers, May Day, National Guard troops, tanks and flowers, Vietnam street execution, politicization of a generation, assassinations, Martin Luther King, JFK, Robert Kennedy, Kent State, the Chicago Convention, mass murders, in MeLai, in Chicago, in a laundromat at random, the social order fell apart, a small country high school in Connecticut where I taught my first year out of college, hair piled high on my head, short skirts. I remember one boy, three years younger than I was, we might have—but I was the teacher. I remember him though, dreamy eyes. If he went to Vietnam, he'd be older than I am by now. The sixties, the Free Speech movement, demonstrators pouring ink in the card catalog at Stanford, protesters saying, *The way to end war is to stop fighting.* Richard Braunstein telling demonstrators at Yale, *I am an artist. I can't stop my work every time the government commits another atrocity.* The young man, what was his name, who returned from Vietnam to tell me, his High School English teacher, about rape, and massacre and *"gooks,"* how there weren't any rules over there. The sixties. Consciousness raising groups all over New Haven, a woman shaped like a gunny sack leaning to me in a Women's Movement meeting, *This is revolution.* Me a few years later telling an employer in Texas our goal was to destroy the fabric of American society. Big blue eyes glaring into mine, wondering if I was kidding. The sixties. A boy in my film class in New Haven who shot super-8 film of himself shooting heroin, tenth grade. 1971. At Legal Aid they said, *Throw it in the fire.* Celluloid smoked, curled, burned. *You know what happens to boys in prison? This*

is evidence of a felony. Burn it. It was my last act as a public school teacher.
Ever. The boy gave me a perfect pencil sketch of the fire, the room, the
arched hallways outside. Gothic American evidence, the sixties, a princi-
pal who fired me for giving students the LA Underground Newspaper version
of Jerry Farber's **Student as Nigger**. You could hardly read it, a mimeograph
of a mimeograph of a mimeograph. The sixties. Washington D.C. on fire,
the Poor People's Campaign. Me, following Jesse Jackson all over D.C. because it was the only place in the city a white woman didn't get yelled at.
Art museums in LA, San Francisco, Chicago, New Haven, New York City,
Boston, Philadelphia, New Orleans, Seattle. Libraries and more libraries.
Living on children's theater. Theater in New York, so magnificent, theater
anyplace else is like organ music on a cheap radio. This man, standing in
the parking lot, eyes sparkling, hair peppered with grey, must have been in
my first class. *I was in your play, Carnival,* he tells me, *I was Gustav.* Me
reeling back to a time I'll never understand, I remember pieces of it, then
all of it, then pieces again, but I can't remember Gustav. Who the hell was
Gustav?

PIE

Ice water. Two silver knives to work through the flour and shortening, add salt. It is an old art. Do not work late into the night, with sleep nipping at your sleeves, you will fall off, wake up at three a.m. to a room full of smoke, two black disks in the oven, bad smell. Do not think about business, or the wave of darkness spreading through the Arts, do not think about depression looming on the horizon or the rhetoric and nonsense our leaders toss into its mouth, or the prospect of revolution in America. Zen. Concentrate on the art of pie. It is an old art. Ingredients spread through the house like a layer of snow, later people say: O, *Pie. Pie. We love pie.* It is a good art. No one will say, *Make this pie with only one silver knife, or no ice, or make it with chalk instead of flour.* Fill pie with ingredients at hand, cans of things, fresh fruit, cheese. Add it to a feast. Eat leftovers for breakfast the next day, the celebration begins again, pie filling the recesses of the body, exhilaration. Pie, it is an old art. If we lose it, infants will wither in their mothers' stomachs, writhe at sunken nipples, men will lose direction, US Steel will manufacture rubber and the pillars of society will flop around like spangles on a half-mast flag. Pie. The planets are lined up—Saturn, Uranus, Mars, Jupiter pull earthquakes, pull poison from beneath the surface. Pie, cut through the mix gently, roll out on a layer of wood and flour, pie. Flute the edges, pour in apples and cinnamon and spices. Pie. Zen. Concentrate on the art of pie. The rites of passage pull us through the gates of depression and war. We shall make pie. Cannot resist. We shall celebrate Christmas, Thanksgiving, the Fourth of July; holidays shall find us traversing the continent in search of heritage. No one makes pie like Mother does. Pie. No one says one pie should represent all pies. Pie is like a thumb print. Some are sour. Pie is silent, making only a light simmering noise as it bakes in the oven. It spreads scent gently into our hearts. There is ceremony as pie is lifted out of the heat. They gather. O, *Pie.* The clutter is swept away, space around pie is brought to sharp focus. Light pours down on pie. Concentrate. The art of pie is an old one. Try to imagine life without it. Like the unveiling of a great painting, breaking a champagne bottle over the bow of a ship going off to sea, the ceremony as a cornerstone is laid, pie. Do not roll the crust too thick, roll gently or the center will unfurl, rub extra flour on the rolling pin every fourth stroke, remember these things. Create pie often so the art is not lost. Do not forget temperature. Cold is essential, then heat. You must have an oven, cannot make pie over an open fire or in a barbecue pit. Be firm with those who insist pie can be made in a crockpot or on the back window ledge of a Pontiac left out in August sunlight. Respect the rules of pie.

Sing a song of six pence/ A pocket full of rye/ Four and twenty black birds/ Baked in a pie./ When the pie was opened/ The birds began to sing—

COMING/GOING

I have noticed how hard it is to go through doors. When someone knocks at my front door, the dog goes into hysterics, barking, or jumping, kissing or rolling on the floor. The child goes into antics, greeting, telling things. If it's a friend there's a hug to engineer and the screen door has to be hooked so the dog doesn't bolt. There isn't room in the front hall for so much commotion, so everyone is stepping on everyone's feet and we're all crowded up together in a knot of greeting, kissing, hugging, tail wagging, jumping, talking and I'm usually shouting *Down!* at the dog or *Be Quiet!* to the child while the guest is trying to enter the house. Entrances at Mother's house are calm. It's leaving she has trouble with. She goes out, comes back in, leaves, returns for something she forgot, starts the car, turns it off, starts it again, makes lists, forgets them. I can't leave my house without going back after something either, the phone rings, I forget what I came back for, the phone rings again, I notice it's fifteen minutes later than it's supposed to be. My son is weird about doors too. When I drop him off at school, he comes back to the car again and again, to give me a hug, to tell me to give his father a hug, to tell me the toy he was sneaking into school in his lunchbox can stay in the car after all. Yesterday it took him seven tries to get from the car to the school door. One friend can't go to sleep if there is a closet door open anywhere in the house. She doesn't want to be attacked by that *weird unconscious stuff* at night when she's asleep.

SHAWL

It is rose wool and grey, a trace of angora in the skein, crocheted, a loose stitch, made to be a scarf, but it stretches. It is a rose shawl, hand made by a woman in a private life-care home in San Jose, California, rows of private rooms the size of large closets for women to move into, traditional women, who sort through houses full of furniture, lives full of china and clothing, nicknacks and children, boiling a lifetime of possessions like hard candy down, down to one room, a one-room-sized collection of things selected to maintain and then end motherhood, a rose shawl. It warms me slightly, the rose colored wool, its softness comforts me, slightly, in spite of the waste it stands for. Women, set aside to die, amid an endless round of formal buffet luncheons, bridge rounds and full dress dinners. The women's home is like a sorority house, but there's no college, just women in an antiquated dormitory, mothers waiting to die, occasionally one crochets a scarf, or afghan. Someone's cousin buys it, or it goes to the infirmary, to be draped across the legs of someone stretched out in clean, comfortable, final prostration. Mother has belonged to this sorority all her life, daughters can join. All you have to do is have free time and believe in God. If you can accomplish that, you can grow old here, and be taken care of, in San Jose, or in a place like it. There's one in every state, rose gardens out front—gorgeous enough to take your breath away. The rose shawl I wear this brilliant October day is beautiful, as Mother was, so many mothers, so many mothers, rose petal faces turned up for sweet cakes and jello. These are the mothers whose sons, fathers, husbands and lovers died violently all over the globe in the 20th Century, to protect us, whose gentle fingers produce this: a rose shawl, in October. What shall we do with these gifts? What shall we do with these mothers?

GOLDEN GATE TRANSIT

On the bus to San Francisco a young man sat next to me in the front seat. He asked the driver where the Presbyterian hospital was, or rather where the hospital was that used to be called Presbyterian Hospital. The name was different now, he said. The driver glanced back at him and shrugged. The boy said he was sure he'd recognize it once he got into the city but he thought a street name or two wouldn't do any harm, might help him get oriented. I handed him a map and read manuscripts as the bus loped and bumped down highway 101 toward the rainbow tunnel in Sausalito, the Bridge and then San Francisco. The young man called out names, trying out the sounds for familiarity: *Clayton Street, Fillmore, Van Ness, Lombard Street, Market Street, Mission, Sacramento, Sutter, Vallejo, California, Geary, Cabrillo, Irving, Ocean Avenue, North Point, Bay Street, Broadway, Grant, Telegraph Hill, Jefferson, Divisidero, Fulton, Grove, Octavia, Pine, Greenwich, 19th Street, Haight, Claremont Boulevard, Funnston, Lobos Point, Great Highway, Park Presidio Boulevard, Stanyan, Willard, Frederick, Knollview, Nob Hill, Saint Francis Boulevard, Portolla Drive, Claremont, Sloat, Merced, San Jose Avenue, Waller, Lincoln Way, Filbert, Union, Leavenworth, Taylor, Sheridan, Harrison, Bryant, Folsom, The Proposed Freeway, Mission, Fremont, Beale Street* (I thought that was in New Orleans), *Spear, Greenwich* (which ought to be New York), *Hyde, Columbus Avenue, McAllister, Gough Street, Divison, Stockton, Clay.* There ought to be a key, I thought vaguely, what if he were sick. It should be possible to find a hospital in San Francisco. He liked the sound of Mission and said that a lot. He liked Divisidero too. At one point I laughed at something I was reading and the boy thought I was laughing at him. *I bet you think I'm crazy,* he said, *going into the City like this, no idea where I'm going.* I told him he was better off than most of us, *At least you know you don't know where you're going.*

SCHIZOPHRENIA

34 years old,
gaunt from the disease
or from the drugs
which help him function,
he wonders
how anyone could
really want to talk
to him on the telephone,
says a broken knee cap,
two metal pins in his leg,
a 26 inch incision
and a hip-to-ankle cast
are *no biggie*
because the pain pills
work,
are nothing compared
to the pain
that attacks his soul.

Schizophrenia,
mental illness.
He was hit by a car
he didn't see,
was crossing the street,
was walking through
the fog he tries
to live in,
sorting internal
and external realities—
mental illness.

O brave heart,
frail body.
O brave human heart.

URBAN SHADOW

I was traveling across a vibrant plain,
green, on a walk that ran alongside a
wide road where cars, buses and trolleys
exchanged in endless chains of motion.
Wires strung up high above the metropolis
connected micro to macro, small to large.

I saw oversized sky scrapers on the far
side of a ravine I recognized from childhood
and the shadows they cast out spread waves of
darkness and desolation—sharp contrast to
bright green healing growing plants.
And I was moving toward the shadow.

The instant I crossed into it
darkness became so vast I lost direction,
froze. It was completely unfinished—
black, empty and cold. It was the rough
shadow of the psyche, of humankind, of winter
solstice, the underside of history.

It was my shadow, a projection from my
soul, my wall, my problem, my chaotic heart,
my instant of terror and I felt it engulf
me in a total emptiness more
powerful than the white light
which I have also seen.

Often since then I have sat curled up,
arms wrapped around knees, and rocked,
aching for something ending, reeling
from shock, trembling in anger at people
I hardly know, crying, shrieking.
I can barely function.

I suppose it was a vision.
I suppose there is a message on the far side

of the darkness I need to understand or
decode. But I have felt defeated
and minuscule since I felt the power of
the shadow, and how cold it is.
I think it can kill me.

I think it is your shadow too.
I think it can kill you and your children
and my children and everything I understand.
I think it is my fault.
I think it is your fault.
I think it has mass and is a tangible
result of logic that shuts down the heart.

BLACK STONE

Sand pours through an hour glass, then out. War gods beckon, Yaweh, God, Allah. Sand shifts on the desert. Is there time to read the Koran? Mohammed was a general. Jesus was a martyr. A Bedouin man's eyes flash, black light. He is smart, a student of the world. His brothers have invited a giant to supper. A bandit has stolen the bank of Kuwait, and the people inside it. Sand blows on the desert. Blood spills on sand, is what it covers. What is the answer? The red-black stone in Mecca, the dark stone, the Kaaba—what is it? The word *cube* comes from a black stone. Four corners, logic, thinking. Arabs invented numbers. In the Middle Ages their culture flourished. Now books are lost, uncatalogued, locked in mosques. Like all children of war gods, these men, with the black flashing eyes, don't know what they know, the black stone, black gold, black flashing eyes. Sand blows on the desert, is what it covers. The boy in my class in America, the boy studying English, his rings flash. The oil is his. You can see it in his eyes. Onyx, sand baked to crystal, gold black, eyes flash, black gold. I want to tell his mother this young man is more precious than oil. I want to tell his mother our sons are more important than countries, or war gods. Watch them laugh—the children are more important than oil. Sand blows, but it cannot cover a woman's passion for murdered children. Nothing covers that. I want to tell his mother that we don't want the oil. I want to tell her my son is more important to me than my car. But the maniac has pointed a gun at her face. The maniac has covered her face with a veil, or just recently uncovered it so that she can hardly speak. Her son is dumbfounded by free women. Sand blows in the desert. Is what it covers. America sent 150,000 men and women there to protect oil, sent 150,000 people four gallons of bottled water a day each, so they could wait on the desert, in a country where a king, in 1987, executed his granddaughter for adultery, half a million gallons of bottled water a day, twenty-two million dollars a day for soldiers and bottled water, *smart* bombs that hit 30% of their targets, bombers, ships, and miscellaneous equipment, all sitting out on the desert, facing off a maniac—thinking it to be something other than ourselves, black gold, numbers, flashing eyes, a million ideas locked in church and the cube.

CLEAR AND CONCISE

With a poet's conciseness he put it together,
dropping into the office where I sat grading papers,
following me from Xerox machine to table, to office, and back.
Have you seen the new grammar book?
There is a chapter about sexist language.
I tell my students to use 'he', he says.
It was good enough for my Daddy. It's good enough for me.

He jokes, but I don't think it funny,
The National Council of Teachers of English recommends
non-sexist language be used by all teachers.
Since when!
Since twenty years ago!

We move from one room to the next,
me trying to work,
him spoiling for debate.

He says his son is in Saudi Arabia
 guarding an aircraft base, a perfect target for poison gas.
What is dangerous is that you can't tell who the enemy is.
They all look alike, he adds and then,
 I told him to shoot first and let God sort out the difference.
That's what we did in Nam.

Excuse me, my Hawk is showing.
I am collating papers for my next class as he continues,
They should send us forty year-olds over.
We'd find a solution. It can't be solved by kids.

With a poet's conciseness he put it together,
sexist, racist, religious and warlike.

He said, *You know me. I'm a recovering reactionary.*
But there's no recovery from that. For any of us.

THERE ARE NO CIVILIANS

Turning and turning in the widening gyre
The falcon cannot hear the falconer
Things fall apart, the center cannot hold
Mere anarchy is loosed upon the world,
The blood-dimmed tide is loosed, and everywhere
The ceremony of innocence is drowned;
The best lack all conviction, while the worst
Are full of passionate intensity.

W. B. Yeates
from *The Second Coming*

Town meetings across America play on public radio, Radio Free America is a groundswell of *No*. A million voices saying, *No*, but the machine is deaf, hard working and passionate, the crazy people own it, children of color bleed into the sand. *No.* A million voices, more, say **No.** Thirty thousand people marching in San Francisco, fifteen seconds on national T.V., then a three minute special: twelve people with yellow ribbons, walking around a flag pole in Iowa—manipulation of reality, the Pentagon News Network. Hands, heavy with anguish, sort paper, feet trudge about homes where hope flickers out, children pulled from college are sent to the desert. Sub-zero winds blast homeless people worldwide, plague ravished people on four continents suffer and then die, *The blood dimmed tide*. We are the beast. Hearts swell heavy to bursting with dumb cynicism, resignation, and denial. An idiot, thick headed and mean, is driving a war machine whose wheels and gears, electronic parts, nuts and bolts are the blood of poor people world around, blood and sweat, blatant violence, the most violent century in history, *the widening gyre*, a beast born, born of every man and woman on the planet, *slouching toward Bethlehem*. I am sick of it. I am fed up with slogans, oration, assassinations, machine guns grazing crowds, America bombing the hell out of third world countries to boost itself out of economic depression. We are the beast. The beast is a machine. Eighty percent of the deaths (they call them casualties) in Vietnam were civilian. There are no civilians, no exemptions. *Casualties? Casual?* The death of someone's father, brother, son, lover, mother, grandmother, grandfather, daughter, casual? There are no civilians, no safe corners isolated by money or culture, no pillows or long wood benches in the lobby where it is safe to nurse an infant—*the center cannot hold.*

A BRICK WALL

The wall was a black shroud, wrapped around her like chain mail, like op-pression, a nightmare. It was made of shadow, impenetrable, her shadow, and it suited her. The wall blocked anything she wanted blocked, her body bled into its vastness, the moon ached and splashed tides against both sides of it. Sun baked mud bricks to a deep green/black sheen like coal. It tow-ered as high as it needed to, into space, past the starship, where starlight was porous like volcanic rock, it tunneled into earth core and spun with the planet. It held fast. It would be incorrect to assume that one man or many built it. It would be foolish to think anyone could take it apart, care-fully assembled, fired, baked and bled to perfection as it was. It was a wall because she wanted it to be one. It was a crust, self encrusted, turned to stone. It was a child running out of chaos who turned to look back, stones dropped around her like a cell, became every cell. It was a wall. It was her protection, her cell. Death could not penetrate it, nor birth, passion or laughter. It was a grid around a girl running fast out of the underworld into light that was razor sharp and full of hatred—one tear, crystal mortar. One heartbeat, a solar bell struck against one tear. It was a wall, it was ego, hu-man dullness drilled into her, built up around her until she became in fact a brick wall.

COPS-OF-THE-WORLD SCHOOL

The classroom is sealed shut. Cool or warm air is summoned from an electronic box on the wall. Windows don't open. It is January 16, 1991. War has broken out in the Middle East. It is 65 degrees and the sun is shining in the capital city of Texas in the United States of America. It is a beautiful day on the planet Earth, except that in a place which used to be called the *cradle of civilization*, twenty-nine nations have agreed to fight over a natural resource which exists on the planet in abundance, but won't for long. It provides energy that is essential to systems that are sealed shut, systems human beings depend on. Human beings could get energy from the sun, which is immortal, but choose to do otherwise. It is January 16, 1991, in the National Security State. A teacher gestures, mouth opens, shuts, student faces wrinkle and blush. They find words to define the American Character: *racist, sexist, arrogant, violent and hard working.* Today, the children are ashamed of their country. Yesterday one of the boys went to war. The day before others disappeared. Today students do not want to sit in a classroom that needs air conditioning on a perfect day in January, perfect, that is except for the fact that the President of the United States has declared war on another third world country, perfect except for the fact that human beings cycle over and over again back to war, war in the name of peace, war in the name of a new world order. Like the war before the last one, WWII, *the war to end all wars,* Operation Desert Storm rains firestorm on people who are—must be—evil. Why else would we do it? Probably we should *just nuke them, it would save lives.* It would save lives? Times like these bring out the best in people, like the man in the market last night: *Did you see those protesters down at the capital? I don't understand where they get off! Don't they watch television? Don't they know what is going on! The President did everything he could do. If he hadn't gone in there it would have been just like Hitler. I just hope that when their house is broken into and their daughter is raped and they call the police, that the police don't come!* Did we educate this young man in a classroom that was sealed shut, or what?

WARRIOR

The warrior
grew out of
a boy
child,
has a thousand
faces,
war paint,
masks,
a grim smile.

His thoughts
are knives.
Even when he speaks
in his most gentle
voice,
there is violence
underneath.

I have seen him in
a thousand white
shirts.
I have seen him
asleep
and bathing.
I have seen him taking
his own son
to warrior school.

I have heard
how he steals into
his daughter's room
late at night
or in the morning
and rapes her,
or steals her power
in more subtle
ways
saying,

Smile for Daddy.
saying,
*The boys must
go to college
first.*

I have seen rows
of him in ceremonial
dress: ministers,
priests, judges,
councilmen, police.

He wears costumes,
weaves a dance
called *law*,
harsh dance,
hundreds of him
stepping in
unison,
stepping and thinking
together
millions of him,
until he mistakes
his thoughts
for truth,
until the most
evil acts imaginable
become,
OK,
acceptable,
commonplace,
heroic.

I have seen the warrior,
thousands of him,
moving together
in a machine more
monolithic than
the factory.

I have seen him turn
the Industrial Revolution
to mass murder,
and before that I have
seen him hunt for
sport,
or rape,
because it is faster
than communication.

I look into the eyes
of my own child,
open,
blinking eyes
full of questions,
open soul
that imprints
everything I do,
think and feel.

The warrior
grew out of a small boy
like my son,
like your sons.

REGRET

tastes
harsh,
like an ulcer
or too much coffee,
like alcohol and aspirin,
too much ibuprofen,
not enough sleep,
anxious shock,
shocking realization
someone is gone,
shut away,
dead,
someone you don't
want to live
without.

MOTHER'S GRIEF

Mother lived with grief
her entire life,
grief for a father
who died of sleeping sickness,
grief for a brother
who died
mid-life,
grief for a son
who died in childhood,
grief of a woman
who lived
for other people.

Mother
was never happy
except
when I behaved.

I hated
the life she planned
for me,
and anyway,
who can behave
well enough
to bring back
the dead?

EXHAUSTION IS MY LOVER

Like the women who have come before, I have taken a new lover. Exhaustion sleeps next to my skin like a thin cloth, I use its retrograde power. Out of the pit of negativity it generates, I search, explore, imagine a different kind of existence, one where energy explodes into the man, spirals back to me enhanced. In the meantime I work three jobs, hang on to the material plane with dull tenacity, listen to the child sound the tuning fork he is, play and stretch enough to be a parent. Exhaustion is my lover, lies with me, pulls me into deepness of center, into the dream place, deeper than that, it pulls me to essence, traces crow feet smile lines around my mouth and eyes, sets a hard opaque glint to my skin, strips me of pretense. I have no time for games, I have no time to waste on dead-end relationships, exhaustion is my lover, is jealous of anything that takes time. Exhaustion and I grow old together, we are energy pulled out of necessity, we are pushed to limits that back off when we attack. Exhaustion and I are tight, like twins, we're giddy and light-hearted. We peel away what doesn't matter, sneak through walls and push existence past boundaries that look impenetrable. Exhaustion is my drug, my opiate, obsession, lover, joy and sorrow, my passion—how sweetly it pulls me down, sleep, luxuriant and peaceful, rich with image, down pillows, sleep—sleep, sleep.

INFIDELITY

He was unfaithful all his life
to one thing or another, to the ideal,
to the song, to perfection.
His days were spent digging in pits

for maintenance, nights were spent wallowing
in the wrong place, in reality instead of dream,
for instance, where he knew he could create mask
after mask, of a god he had been unfaithful to.

Without meaning harm,
he was unfaithful his entire life,
to the god of music, to the god of art,
creating a half-life when he knew
perfection was possible.

When he closed his eyes, and dreamed
into timelessness, when he leaned back
and looked deep into space, into the universe,
he knew he had been unfaithful to love.

He did it by being faithful to friends,
family and work. He wasn't alone.
He did it by turning away from everything
that could have wrapped him in infinity.

But he was too tactical for dreams, too solid for perfection.
He lived in a hurricane of unsolved conflicts,
crawled and did not fly, worked for money and not love.
He was unfaithful to himself.

POSTAL CLERK

She was rearranging
the mail,
struggling with
pressure sensitive
labels.
Her tongue cracked
with pungent glue cuts,
her fingers were worn
slick from stuffing
envelopes.

She was testing
and spinning
and aching,
blasted
mid-life
open—
when
the man moved
to Denver.

As she sat in the mail room
listening to customers
a single stream of tears
ran out of her right eye.

Later
back home,
she saw herself go up in
smoke,
ignite,
arms turned to fire,
orange, red, yellow
flames leapt
out of her chest,
neck,
breasts,
from her lungs,
everyplace!
Fire.

THE CHILD CALLS TO A PARENT TOO UNHAPPY TO CARE

I want to walk with you
in the park
I want my life to be full
of your
love
falling down around
me—
over me
thru.

Please,
learn how to reach
out
of your pain.

Please,
remember how
to hold me
in your arms—
laugh,
laugh with me,
play,
play with me
play, with me, play.

THE BIRD DIED

My son,
bicycling,
found a
dying crow
and brought
it home
to me.

It was
hollow,
light boned.
It stretched
its feet
and beak
but
couldn't
crow.

I held
it in my hands—
soul left.

OF

I have seen the eternal Footman hold my coat, and snicker,
And in short, I was afraid.

T.S. Eliot
from *The Love Song of J. Alfred Prufrock*

NEWS

The worst possible
news,
dreams, nightmares,
everything rushing into
a vat,
the derelict
cut loose,
robbing
our house
of Father.

Cancer.
Fatal.
Soon.

MAPS

John said cancer fed on his mother for eight years, each time taking more and more of her, so that eventually she was almost unrecognizable, the medicine she took, he said, would have killed any three of us. He said in spite of all the change, in spite of how diminished she had become, the essence was there, that she was still *Mom*, still mother to five children and when she died it was *Mom* they cried for, not the sick one. Jane said Hospice helped her mother the last months. From first diagnosis, Rosalie knew it would kill her, the point of choice was how and when. It was death by strangulation, cancer wrapping itself in a tight sheath around her lungs. She said cancer therapy was an art, that cures are tools which destroy as they repair, that there are trade offs, each person has to choose their path. Rosalie said she didn't want to be helpless and got suicide pills but she didn't use them. Instead she talked herself out, talked to Jane, Jane beside her, mother/daughter, a vibrant circle of power and love and death. Jane said Hospice helped her understand what has happening. *What does she need to eat for?* the nurse said, *She's dying.* I have seen Father go through stages of denial, anger, grace. I have seen him crack jokes and have watched his mind dance around the ones who think they're taking care of him. I have seen him carry a book into surgery. I have held him as he flew into the dark hole of terror, helplessness, narcotics spinning through his veins, numbing cancer's progress as it bored into his nerves. Karla says we settle into the waiting time, that it's like waiting for a baby to be born. Nature. They go like they come, in pain, at their own pace. They gather light, fold themselves in darkness, reach out one last time, then go. These words, given to me by friends, are maps. I hold them as Father held the book regardless of the fact that he was being taken to surgery where everyone knows it is too dark to read.

COMMUTER

For awhile
I was a commuter
between Texas
and Northern California.

Father dying,
I traveled
back and forth,
to be with him,
play a game of scrabble,
joke, talk, listen to him read,
read to him, help Mother,
spend time with Sister.

I worked on planes,
in airports and on the bus,
reading manuscripts,
grading papers, writing and
planning interrupted only
slightly by the landing
or take-off of planes,
a change in elevation
no more significant
than the ring of a telephone
or going downhill
to the mail box.

The continent split—
father on one side,
son on the other, home,
home—
two homes,
two tangles of passion
and need.

Home.
We split families
the way we split atoms,
a glow of light—
then out.

CANFIELD

We play cards.
Or rather he plays cards,
as he has been doing for the last year—
a kind of solitaire
called Canfield.

He says when he was in college
he used to buy a deck of cards
for $50 and play all night.
If you could put all the cards up
in sequence, you won $200.

I laugh at him.
Grandmother, who did not allow
card playing, would be horrified
at your gambling, and you
were supposed to be studying.

I did study, he tells me,
and I tutored other people
who were having trouble,
and the money they paid me,
I used to buy cards
for Canfield.

I point to a run he's missed.
He fixes it.
I point to another one.
He fixes that too.

The next one
he finds himself
and says—
Beat ya!,
then he tells me
where every card
in the deck is.

So I find him,
the man with the fine mind,
the one who can't stand
to be told anything,
let alone that he is dying.

It's a solitary run.
You play against the house.
You can't win.
Eventually you can't even play.

RESPITE

After the heater blew up
in Jimmy's face
and he was covered
with burns, immobile,
confined in bandages
and pain,
alcohol and drug free
for the first time
since Junior High School,
he kept asking
for a break—
an hour or two off,
away from the hospital,
away from the pain,
the immobility,
so he could go to his favorite
restaurant, EATS,
and have a marguerita,
fresh broccoli and fish.

He promised to come back
and be sick again
after just an hour,
even forty-five minutes.

So it is with me.
I cast about for respite
as Father slumps
to death.

I FIND IT MAKES ME ANGRY

that people
make demands,

that children
roam the streets, untended,

that the man
next door is a child molester,

that there is
tragedy and ignorance and idiocy here,

and that Father
is leaving

me on an insane planet—
no one to help.

PUPPIES

Mother,
Megan and I
were
like puppies
waiting
in the exact
spot
the mother
was last seen
when
they wheeled
Father
in for surgery.

The nurses
set up
chairs
for us
in the hall
outside
the operating
room
when they realized
we weren't going
to move
one inch
until
we
got Father
back.

100 YEAR SHAY

Like the poem
by Whittier,
Father fell apart
after holding
everything together
for all of us,
all at once
he
unraveled,
died
of exhaustion,
a three-month fast,
pneumonia,
pancreatic cancer,
jaundice,
paralysis,
intestinal blockage
and a
collapsed lung.

His vision failed,
legs and feet stopped
obeying commands.
He couldn't swallow.
He said,
I'm like the 100 year shay.

There wasn't any hope.
There was just death,
harrowing decay,
a stripping away
of layer after layer
of personality
and health.

He was gentle.
Light glowed around him,
then disappeared,
and he was gone
to ash, bonedust.

ELIOT

The day before he died, Father couldn't move from bed, swallow or even turn to one side. His breath rattled—brittle voice of death. He quoted T.S. Eliot: *In the room the women come and go, speaking of Michelangelo,* a bit of resonant nonsense? perhaps. I went to find the book. *And would it have been worthwhile? It is as if a magic lantern threw the nerves in patterns on a screen:/ I grow old. I grow old./ I shall wear the bottoms of my trousers rolled.* Lines in a poem about art, a poem about suddenly finding yourself old, about dying, about accepting death, not resurrection, not eternal anything, just disintegration, things falling apart, self falling apart. *I have heard the mermaids singing, each to each./ I do not think that they will sing to me.* Father coughed as I gave him morphine mixed with apricot juice, said, *Breathe carefully,* and began to slowly count, *and one, and two.* He fell into the rhythm, and was hypnotized to sleep, a sleep in which he died. The air that came from his lungs was torrid, decayed, was death. It was already there, inside, waiting for his spirit to go. Daily life moved slowly around his final breath. When the preacher came, except for where the electric blanket had warmed it, the body was cold and was not him. Mother, Megan, Father Jimmy and I stood around the bed. Father Jimmy prayed, but my father didn't believe in Father Jimmy. He believed in life, and died unreconciled.

FATHER FIXED THINGS

In the garage, neatly arranged on hooks he twisted by hand into slats of wood that ran between wall studs, Father kept a small array of tools—wood clamps in many sizes, tapes of different types. Screws arranged by size he had saved in baby-food jars that were as old as we were. He nailed the jar tops to the undersides of shelves so that to get inside you had to turn the jar, and not the lid which remained still. We used to ask him how many Fathers it took to *unlid a screw.* He fixed broken furniture, shoes that heels had come loose from, toys that came apart, cracks in things, garden tools, window screens, door latches, anything that promised future use, and some that didn't, he fixed. It was a matter of pride with him for things to be clean, neat and in repair. He was glad for things to fix. Weekends found him puttering in the garage, taping things, applying glue. He was particularly fond of tape. We found it everyplace—on suitcases, in bureau drawers, on the backs of kitchen cabinets, on jewelry boxes, on shoes. Packages from him were a glory of tape. Father liked it when things worked. He hated bickering and arguments about small things, like time, or privilege. He liked to wander the universe of his poet's mind in peace. He hated it when we fought, or vied for his attention. He didn't know how to fix us, so he'd wander out to the garage where materials were more to his liking. When he died, a trail of broken things stretched into my mother's life, sister's mind, for instance. But who can fix a thing like that? He had been patching her together for years, but Mother didn't have the right touch. So she worked on smaller things. Once an outdoor sprinkler set for 3:00 a.m. broke and sent water in a perfect stream from the bed outdoors into the one Mother was sleeping in. She fixed that. Alone, at 3:00 a.m., in her nightgown, barefoot in the garden, she fixed it and said afterwards maybe it was too much for her, living alone, without anyone to help. It's not like having to take out the garbage, or doing the million things you can plan for. It's that things keep breaking and Father's not here to fix them anymore.

SHROUD

We met her plane,
a little late.

Mother, looking
anxiously
into a river
of faces
for me,
was
wearing
Father's shroud.

It was as if
he hovered,
just behind
and to the left
of her,
then vanished,
leaving her
with me.

How is that possible?
I ask myself,
and disbelieve
the evidence
of my own eyes.

IMITATOR

Father,
when
he wants
to make me laugh,
your grandson
pulls
his pants
highwasted up,
puts on your hat,
and walks,
one leg swung out
funny,
singing,
Grandpa's back.

WILLIAM'S ROSE

He liked roses,
watched them climb the back fence, pruned
and cut back bad spots, knew each day
the stage of every flower, bud to petal fall.

He liked roses,
stood with his pipe, blew smoke above their faces,
up and out towards the Santa Rosa mountains,
rose colored in the afternoon, like their name.

He and the roses
watched the fog roll in and out mornings and evenings,
he watched from the back fence, with the roses,
liked to stand with them, and think.

He cut yellow roses
when I came to visit, brought them in the house,
although Mother didn't like the smell,
it made her eyes tear.

He liked roses,
Mother didn't. She didn't like poetry either. Told
me to stop writing and get a real job, like Father did,
said he did it because he loved us.

I bring yellow roses
in the house still, put them in a cut glass vase, set
it on his table, feel less lonely and insist
my words are William's rose.

GRACE

THE POETS

I reckon, when I count at all,
First Poets—then the sun—
Then Summer—then the Heaven of God—
And then the list is done.
But looking back—the first so seems
To comprehend the whole—
The others look a needless show,
So I write Poets—All.
Their summer lasts a solid year,
They can afford a sun
The East would deem extravagant,
And if the final Heaven
Be beautiful as they disclose
To those who trust in them,
It is too difficult a grace
To justify the dream.

Emily Dickenson

SHIPWRECKED IN THE PRESENT

Crashed here, for centuries, a dull thud,
and then this landscape,
sand.

To see the world in a grain of sand—
                              (Blake)

Pieces, particles of
sand.

Shipwrecked here.

A man loping into my kitchen
saying,
I am one of his angels.

It is true.
I am.

Here. Now.
I am here.
No hope of something else.

Do I like it?
All this sand, slats of the bow,
almost covered over,
hot wind.
Soon we will forget the voyage.

Exhaustion,
is it an emotion?
It fills the empty spaces
of the soul,
sand.

I recall a flood,
remember fast currents.
I saw life drain out of my father,
drop by drop,

we raced midstream
through catastrophe.

The river stopped
here
in sand,
pieces of matter
polished by wind and water,
dry,
blow across
broken boards,
pieces of me,
buried
here
now
here
now
here
now.

*"How stale and unprofitable seem to me
all the uses of—"*
                        (Hamlet)
One year ago does not exist,
or tomorrow.
Here.
Now.
Shipwrecked in the present.

GRACE

appears.
She is wearing lavender
cotton pants and a leopard shirt,
has a bundle
of papers in
her arms,
wants me to
get some work done
free and fast.

It doesn't feel much
like Grace,
but it's her,
a country woman who lives
in eight centuries
simultaneously
whose nonsense
is brilliant,
who pulls garbage
out of her crotch,
whose temple is
a caliche pasture
that blooms roses
and old bed posts.

DIAMOND

Out
of the diamond
I hear myself
rising
sheer cut
and gleaming,
water/clear
and singing.

The song that
I am—
a reflection,
inverted,
carved backwards,
in razor sharp
spiral,
the soul/light
is radiant;
it blinds me
almost
to the rest
of my life.

The diamond
is flashing.
The woman
is watching.
The woman
is shining.

The song of it
vibrates,
a silk threaded
listening
cuts through
dimension.

Diamond light,
halo,
diamond hum,

passion,
diamond song,
mystery
diamond man,
laughter,
like sunlight
after midnight
like olives,
like tears
that cut
deep,
or pleasure,
or breath.

The art
wants me
now,
I can hear
it
but the crystal
flies back
like a bat
living backwards
so far
in the past
its magnificent
fire
burns out
or
I lose it
again
(how could
I have
done that?)
as the clatter
of everything
swirls
like a dragon
and
I rise
from the diamond

like a lake
that's turned over,
disheveled
and cloudy,
long hair
matted
like snakes
who've been swimming
in the galaxy
to outgrow
their skin.

And I search
for a skin
I can live in
again,
still and again,
the song
of it spiraling
like skill saws
and concrete
in a matrix
someplace inside
me, a cave
or a mine.

The lists wait unfinished
perfect, in my absence.

A small boy
a small boy
calls out *Mommie—*
calls out *Mommie!*

Or I swim
in a cold
emerald pool.

The diamond.
The diamond.
The diamond.
The diamond.

THE CREEK

Go down and look Helen told me. Mother was 76, Helen 82, too old to climb down to the creek. So I found my way alone down to the water where we used to play as children. When father couldn't stand what was happening to him, I asked Helen what he loved, how to remind him of something good, to put next to the pain in his mind. *Remind him of the creek, of when he was a boy,* she said. So I told him, *You don't have to stay here. Go back to the farm, to the creek, listen to the water run over grey stones, coal colored water. Remember the creek.* That's how in his last few hours, some part of him came here. Sound first bonded me to the creek, and then plants, ferns and wild comfrey, wild flowers—*Trillium, Lilly of the Valley* (for which I am named), Violets, *Blue Gentians, Hepatias, Anemone*—and the deep carpet of leaf mulch, like walking on a mattress. Sinking ankle deep into this once, I reached for a walking stick that snapped and set me tumbling into the leaves and sticks and the rich smell of forest earth. I was listening to the sound of water running over stone. I was enchanted by the darkness of the forest, by splashes of sunlight that came though what Father called *windows* in the trees. Father said they cut windows in the forest to warm up the creek water where it flowed into a concrete swimming pool which Grandfather built alongside the main part of the creek. Father said it didn't help, that creek water was cold enough to wake the dead. Perhaps it had. I asked Helen what the creek was called. She said it didn't have a name, that it had just always been called *the creek.* I wonder if the land remembers us, knows our souls or the rhythm of our footfall. I wonder and am filled with wonder by this place that doesn't need a name.

IDA

for Ida Mae Roberts Collins Smith
July 15, 1896—August 1, 1992

The old people
unfold
like moth wings
hovering
over winter grain.

Their
tears are the water
of
communion.

As
we listen
to their lives,
our
own
sing.

EVEN IN CHINA?

The child is sick. It is temporary, but what if it was not? How do you parent a child who is dying? My parents did it. I remember nothing from that time except their pain. When the sun is brilliant and the world is clicking inside and outside my skin, and there are things to do!, how do I achieve patience, patience as the child sleeps, cries, refuses food because it makes him sick, how quickly he falls to exhaustion, saying *Mommie, I think I going to die.* How can I focus on work when I am tiptoeing in to see if he is breathing? Mother says I have to be more patient, but I am a different kind of woman, impatient, for one thing. I fall into pools of love and grief each day, can set the clock by them. Walking along the river I watch the child on his bike chase ducks. His feet pedaling, pedaling, he speeds up, airborn sailing, bicycle and all, off the bluff into the creek, ducks flapping and splashing, cold north wind. Tears and shock. *Mommie, this doesn't feel good!* Another day he races downhill toward a train, hits brakes at the exact instant his tires hit tree roots, flies head-over-heels, lands sprawling, people on the train wide-eyed, close enough to touch him. The child is interesting. And I am interesting and I've run into trains myself. Mother is right, I need to be more patient but my nerves are shot. Mother loved one man her entire life. That is inconceivable to me. Today the mail brings a letter from her containing an article about Salmonella, along with a note that says, *Here is an article for you. Dad says you won't read it.* I read part of it, how our kitchen sponges are full of germs, and mayonnaise and chicken eggs are suspect, how food poisoning is mistaken for flu, how you can put dish rags in the microwave oven and it will blast germs the way it would explode a pigeon. Mother cleans her kitchen with bleach to kill germs. We don't do that. We dodge moving trains. The child tells me he can't keep chicken soup down but he thinks ice cream might work. I stretch out on the sofa, the child curls up on top of me. *I saw the end of the world. Oh,* I say. *It is a gate but you can't go through it because you will fall into space.* Silence and then—*Do all children have to behave? Yes,* I tell him. *Even in China? Yes, even in China the children must learn to behave.*

ONE DREAM

for Jessie Rhiannon Whitebird
July 12, 1983—February 27, 1989

Every dream in the universe
lives
in the heart
of a dying child
as the mother, the father
tiptoe in,
watch
her
toss, turn,
mumble, cry out!
or laugh.

She is dreaming
a lifetime,
living moments
condensed,
so one swing ride
in the hammock
on the back porch
is all
swing rides,
one wedding
is all weddings,
one birthday
is all birthdays,
one trip to the park
is all trips
to the park.

We live in the wake
of her grace,
this child of death.
As she heals,
we float ecstatic.

If she dies
we will have seen
evil's most
irate and pointless
face.

There is no harder
grace
than a child
who lives
a whole lifetime
in one dream.

MAKING PEACE WITH THE CHILD

A young girl, white/gold hair, white leather shoes, standing in a farmyard, there are sheep, and a collie named *Tinker*. It is summer in Pennsylvania, in the mountains, air is sweet, creek water rushes out of snow just past the meadow. How to prepare a child for the way death stops everything, Mother's smile, for instance, Father's grace. A vast silence implodes, then travel, a new house and school in the Midwest, harsh weather, harsh people, no cousins, no pets. Trains belch steam, take Father to the city, the magnet, a dark canyon, Chicago. And the lake, waves taller than the child, water like blue ice, or green. At school the girl stopped trying to please, acted up, read upside down. Then the sixties, blood on the streets, assassinations, bombs in the laundromat, CIA and IRS audits, they even tapped her phone. Who could have prepared her for the way all revolutions became one revolution. Or for the way men loved her out of existence. She wanted to save something. She was tired of children being ruined, she was tired of bad ideas, poison ones like religion. She thought if one child could heal, it would prove that there was hope, a fine thread, a loophole to pull civilization through. How to make peace with her, the child in the farmyard, the one swaying in tall grass, the one whose first steps were a dead run away from grief. Is there an idea, a principle, an echo, song, chord, god, goddess, is there something I can teach her, the child knee deep in silence, to reclaim her heart, so she can love again, live, breathe deep, be energized by beauty, not drained? How to make peace with his absence, the boy who left without saying good-bye, was too sick to speak, and they were afraid of contagion. Contagion? The girl was healthy as wind, mistrusted illness, refused it. The boy died, and the parents left with him, fell into a hole of despair. How to make peace with her, the child, someplace to start, the rest can come later, if one heart can heal, others can too, a small girl standing in farm grass, me.

MEDITATION

You are at the center of a circle. Reach out and touch its cool perimeter. It expands. Move through the corridors of a building, cool air whirls about your feet. The circle expands. You are wandering across an open field. The emerald grass of spring opens a thousand new sensations to your heart, the circle expands. Balance on the borders between countries. Different languages buzz between your ears, you hear laughter in a thousand tongues. The circle expands. Ride the tops of clouds, see the morning star from the other side. Feel the cold black joy of the universe, stride on stars like gravel on a country road. You are free here. Soar.

Soaring, tug at the perimeter of the circle to call it gently back through centuries of space, through a million images and dreams, gently pull at the rim of the circle. It draws elegantly to your call. Down like a cone it spirals through the laughter of a million clowns, through mosaic fantastic temples of the world's religions, down to a creek bed in the mountains where trout are waiting to be caught, down to the valley of your spirit and from there to the corridors of habit where you live and breathe and dance, moving here, moving there, moving always from this single central point.

SHATTERED GLASS

for Glee and Gerry

In the shape of a charm,
shamrock, clover,
amethyst at the center,
struggling to be,
enclosed,
it is stained glass.
It is glass art
made out of
shattered glass
that came from
the windshield of
a car that veered
off a city street
in Sacramento,
rolled and crashed,
rolled again,
then stopped—
smashing the
teenage girl
who had been driving—
crushed lungs,
crushed arm,
resuscitated by medical
technology for six weeks,
then allowed
to die,
the struggle,
she could not—
was too weak to hold.

And the father
mourned,
and in mourning
showed me
how to cast light
into
the broken pieces

of my own
grief,
as I led him
also,
into the circle
of survival
where we try to
understand
why we are alive
instead
of those more
innocent,
more pure—

And the woman
whose love
for
him is a gleaming
puzzle,
picked up pieces
of safety glass
from
the side of
the city street
in Sacramento,
formed it
into a medallion,
a difficult
and struggling
sculpture—
tears
flooding every
part
of the
creative act.

It hangs
in his
workplace,
and I cry
when I look

at it—
a difficult
and elegant
glyph—
acceptance.

In the next room
is a sign that says:

There are no problems
that do not contain gifts.
We seek problems because
we need the gifts they bring us.

We say that we do not
want any more gifts,
and light shines through
shattered glass.
I can hardly look.

FIRST RACE

Father, I wish you could see our house, high on a hill. We look down at lights sparkling up around us and feel prosperous in spite of obvious contradictions. I wish you could have seen this house. It's like the one in California. We watch the sunset and are comfortable. The furnishing isn't much, but I still have Great-Grandmother's library table, and Grandpa's trunk, and the Sleepy Hollow chair and your old bookshelves, and the Ansonia Clock, and books, and more books, and the flute. I wish you could have visited us here. We're on a bluff above cold water like we were in the house in the mountains. I still swim every day in cold water. We walk too, uphill, it's good exercise. I've missed you and even though I refuse to admit you're really not here, there is something settled about me now you never saw, or never spoke of if you saw it. I keep my own archives, the strange magazines, the new books pile up here and are less carefully packed away than when you had them. I still read murder mysteries all the time, have found a new writer, Ellis Peters is her pen name, she writes medieval murder mysteries. They're great. John still works with his hands, blunt strong fingers, like Grandpa, like the blacksmith, and his laugh is full, like yours. Father, I wish you could have seen us here because you'd know we're fine. I wish you could see the child. He's smart and funny, talented and independent. It's noisy here. No one will ever stop talking. We all talk at the same time so it's a mine of absurdity, like home. Yesterday the child ran a race along the river. John watched him come in last. It was the first time he'd run a mile and the first time he'd run a race. John said he didn't seem to even notice he was last. Later the child told me he'd stopped to get a drink. I asked if there had been a line. He said there was. He said he'd stopped again to help a child who threw up. He said the other children were laughing so he stopped to help. I taught him to run the race like that, and you taught me. Father I wish you could see us here and know we're fine.

RADIO MAN

for John Aielli

4000 psychic telegrams, 8000 feet, 80,000 toe nails, relating to—every fifteen minutes, 4000 people, 24,000 smile lines in a conglomerate American face, 8000 eyes light, minds flow, tuned to—a kind of mental note. 4000 noses, and the greatest one of all—like Beethoven's ear trumpet, mime face, strangeness, old knowledge, and a voice, music everyplace, gymnastics of the throat and teeth. 28,000 teeth, 4000 tongues and an idea, like eating a banana made out of banana flavoring. Imagination implodes, 8000 ears tuned to mind, tuned to coincidence, radio, tuned to radio. I first heard the Beatles in a small college pub in Indiana, you, playing *I wanna hold your hand* in Kileen, Texas. I first heard Beethoven in a truck driving across open range in Montana, you, playing *I wanna hold your hand* in Kileen, Texas. I first heard the Beatles, and on, and on, ricochet, idea/sound, bounce and splash, splash, third eye. 4000 third eyes, spirit/dance, spiral, spirit/time, eternity, an Eon—hand over mouth, but look it's only music. No revolution in that, just spin, spin and improvise. You talk to us as if I were one person, but we are a trillion strands of hair, more strands of fool than that, one face, always turned side/slant, for breath, mid-crawl. 4000 swimmers in the ocean of a universe that sets side/long vision straight/all jumbled up and elegant, like waves, water dropping off the forearm. Breathe in—air waves, high tech water, from a stone, of course it is a charm. You talk to us as if I were one person but we have 8000 eyes, receive, receive sound/mind. And art is just a high tech cube where virtuosity cavorts.

NO

is a resounding
word,
difficult to hear—
even
gentle No's
grate against
spirit
flying to
completion
in
the wrong
direction.

No
is a resounding
word.

No—
free spirit
of the child
directed to
acceptable
behavior.

Yes.
yes—
say YES
to the child
to me
to yourself.

YES,
  yes, to the dance
  yes, to the light
  yes, to the magic

  and,
  yes, yes to the fall.

THE WHITE LIGHT

I saw it,
the week my sister nearly
died,
was praying
the only way
I know, by
diving
deep into my soul,
for power,
and sending it
to her.

I was nearly asleep
when the white light
poured through me.

I saw it—
and knew
she would heal.

How hard,
the white light's
blessing is,
slow,
faltering across
decades,
centuries.

I saw it again
a few weeks ago,
a swirling spin
of water/light,
white,
clear,
and brilliant.

It was a bridge
that mixed
with mercury,

like thought,
and fanned out
like a delta
at the mouth
of an
imagined
river.

Yesterday,
it was
a
spinning core
of light
that drew me
in, then
let me
out again.

I awoke
at twilight,
disoriented
and
exhausted.

It means change
and it means power.

It means that we
are going to be
all right.

HOME

He wanted to be free enough to follow art, or love
or work or anything, no matter where
the energy took him.
He wanted to be strong enough
to tend the fire at the center of the family
in absentia. He wanted to be fair,
to meet changes head on. He wanted change.
He wanted to grow.
He wanted everyone to get along in peace.

What happened was the opposite of what he wanted.
The energy that took him away from home exploded.
The fire at home flared out of control,
the child erupted, refused in her effective child way
to be calm about father going anyplace without her,
and the woman at home rekindled his love for her.

He cried, was angry, cried some more
and reshouldered the burden of a life he chose
before he realized actions have long-term implications.
The only casualty was love,
The flower that opens in spite of warnings to fall
to the center of the planet, hide there, hide.

The casualty was only love.
He wasn't a romantic so it didn't really matter,
anyway there was love at home, as much as he could stand.

BONFIRE

I might have missed it,
a party in the country, appealing but—no time,
so I might have missed it, the meaning of the great bonfire,
 children playing in a tame river, ankle deep
to last year's sixty foot rise, volley ball on the flood plane,
an autumn feast. I might have missed the point.

The man has cancer, fast growing and dangerous.
A child asked, *Why do you have funny hair?*
Because I do, the man answered and then said,
I know that answer is not going to satisfy you,
or me either, but that's the reason.

We didn't talk about cancer, though we have,
but this was a party and if Annie hadn't stopped
this morning to return things I would have missed the point
of the feast, festival, harvest rite, a great bonfire, twilight,
a mild afternoon, friends gathered by the river,
life force pushing back darkness,
a woman gathering the powers of earth, water,
fire and air, gathering a community together for support,
to gather strength for one hell of a fight for life,
flames jumping out of a stone circle set on dirt.

RITUAL

Love
is absolute
and free, in
love
we
are as strong
as
we need to
be

When the father ages, let him fall to finality,
when the son demands a breast long dry,
find different nourishment, independent life, for instance,
when the lover falls to silence, leave him to his own confusion,
when the brother falls away, send him off with love,
even if your heart is ripped open, even when your body aches,
even when your work flies apart,
let them go,
let them all go.

Their images of you jangle,
you cannot sing if you give your breath away,
cannot live with anyone every instant,
there is no freedom for a woman in a world of men
if they are all inside you.
Clarify, let go.

At high noon on a sunlit day,
gather an image for every man you have loved,
if it takes time,
allow it.

Dried rose petals for the beautiful father, how
your girl heart loves—
cries as he grows old,
let him go,
go with love.

For the boy child,
crepe paper and a plastic cup.

Mothers love sons without masks, with keys that unlock
the universe, send him out to play.
Let him go,
go with love.

Even if the brother falls to madness or death,
if he abandons home, leaves holes in your life,
let him go.
Let him go with love.

Remember each one, name an image:

> *Carve a strip of wood*
> *a folded sheet,*
> *piece of gold,*
> *piece of paper,*
> *toy,*
>
> *a picture*
> *of the pope,*
> *piece of shroud,*
> *piece of music,*
> *a feather.*

Choose the images with care.
Wrap them in white paper, carefully, crunch up white paper,
find an altar where fire can unfold, any way it wants to.

Watch the images go up in smoke, watch white paper
turn black, unfold like a charred book, layer after layer
disappearing
to ash.

Do not look to see which image held against fire,
do not accept messages from ash, luxuriate in the light
fire makes.
Absorb the glow.

> *listen:*
> *a wren, small, brown*

and alive
sings outside
the gate,
perched
on the front eve.
It is your song.

Let the men go free.
When they return, (they come back because they need you)
greet each with as much truth as you can, stretch and grow
into the power of the man
inside the woman,
then let him go.

Let him go,
let them all go,
go with love.

YELLOW—

two lemons
clasped
in
a child's
hands
on a
foggy
morning
in
Northern
California:

smell
like
YELLOW

MIGRATION

To understand bird languages,
swallow a snake.
Carry a hawk tongue
under your own.

Soaring.
Stuffed birds in the house fly away with good fortune. The *robin's* breast is red with the blood of *Christ*. Grind up dry hummingbird, feed it to the woman you love and she will never leave. *Vultures* are all female. To impregnate themselves, they turn backside to the wind. Three years later they give birth. The *phoenix* lays an egg of myrrh in a nest of cassia and incense, then dies. From her bones springs a worm which turns into a *phoenix*. To the *golden hawk*, feed scraps of meat. Do not sneeze in its presence, or you will die. *Buzzard* feathers brush away evil. *Peacock* feathers burn embryo out in miscarriage. *Maat* is the female manifestation of *Toth*, master of law, inventor of speech. Her name means flute, which makes the throat inhale breath. The bird that made milk was hidden, then let out, then stolen but returned, saved the children from a storm, stole them, returned some, married one, made the wind with its wings, stirred up the water, so the fisherman stole it. The *jacksaw* flew off with the ring of the Archbishop of Rheims. The *bats* of Babylonia are the bird-souls of the dead. When Solomon was traveling in the desert, the *hoopoe bird* sheltered him from sunfire. *Zeus* came to Leda in the form of a swan. The *cock of the rock* makes a magical dance, brings the rain. *Red bird*: fire, lightening and blood. Stare into the yellow eye of the *curlew* and jaundice will travel from your body to its. The *oyster-catcher* is benevolent. The white bird in flight makes the sign of the cross. The *barnacle goose* is hatched from a shell fish. The *quail* rides the back of a crane over water. The *osprey* hypnotizes the fish that it catches. The shaman in trance explodes into birdsong. The universe hatched from an egg spawned from the mud in the Nile which is the hidden but eternal name of the sky. The *Goddess of Whirlpool* drew into her body *Quetzalcoatl*, poured in pulque, mist of agave, mushroom, his heart burned up and ascended as morning star. The cult of *sky-hero* is made of the heroes of dreaming. Ignorant of science, the *rainmakers* roll their stones and are thunder. Bird-souls fly out of spirit/time into life. Shooting stars are the recent dead flying in and out of skyworld. Hawaii emerged from the sea when *Great-Bird* descended and laid down an egg. Two *pigeons* flew back and

forth across the water until a blade of grass appeared and dry land followed. The *simurgh* of Persia bore great rain-bearing wings to the desert. The *roc bird* swoops into the Valley of Snakes, brings back lumps of meat to which diamonds adhere. *Zeus* rode an *eagle*. *Venus* rode a *goose*. *Skanda* rode a *peacock*. *Kama* rode a *parrot*. Wing-footed *Mercury*. *Jesus* flew up to the heavens at baptism. *Ravens* were ridden in and out of hell by witches in Europe. The song of a *whale* speeded up is the same as a bird call. *Odin's ravens* gathered the news. A *woodpecker* heard on the right is a good omen, on the left beckons evil. A white bird flying into your house portends death.

> *To understand bird languages,*
> *swallow a snake.*
> *Carry a hawk tongue*
> *under your own.*

JUGGLER

The woman is juggling glass beads. She does not know how to juggle. She is dropping them and some break. Laser shafts streak out of a slate tower at the center of each bead. A pyramid of light that weaves sky down, dances overhead. One bead is full of coins: ancient ones, new ones, silver, gold ones, wood ones, stone ones, quicksilver ones, ones that are engraved, some are magic. The beads are spheres. They explode from spirit world. She is trying to balance them. One bead is crisp with child song, sharp with child passion, the stone is feathered and complicated: images stretched through hard wood, alive. Some beads are metallic, one is clicking and bouncing around the wheel on a roulette table: 0,7,14,21,0. In one bead a goddess is chanting, creating the universe as she dances with a large turquoise serpent: *Venus, Isis, Gaia, Guadalupe, Hera, Diana, Chicomecoatl, Yemonja, Amaterasu, Nu'ah, Nisaba, Luna, Kore, Matt, Rhiannon, Changing Woman, Themis, Nuith, Lilith, Atremis:* woman of a thousand faces. The beads expand, contract, are moons that blaze halos around the head of anyone who's holy. One bead is a tear, liquid, volatile, a universe of rage, the fluid heart of woman sacrificed. The beads are powerful and she can hardly hold them. They slip through outstretched arms, roll down naked skin like drops of water in a sunlit shower. In one bead a fierce stranger—blue eyes mirror a chaotic heart, pure light catches images of her in primary color, soft blue wool, a shadow full of explosions, this bead is a grenade. And the beads are gemstones. The woman is making chains for icons to dance on, a light touch against the chest, heartbeat. And the beads are marbles and the woman is a child, dutch boy hair cut and before that long gold braids. The child is playing alleys on the sidewalk, marbles catch sunlight, spin. For an instant she is at peace, the spheres are balanced, the pattern is elegant:

> *tinkle of glass*
>   *br*
>   *eak*
>   *ing.*

And one bead is a carpenter, Taurean and steady, head turned to bronze earth, leaf mulch, smell of fish, sea air, eyes full of jokes, a man who can wear elegant or sweat soaked clothing—taste of salt. In one bead are voices, women's voices, clear and singing, passionate, joyful, wailing, voices that sing in cycles, that spin to revolution, men's voices join in too. The woman is juggling glass beads, she tosses some too high, some crack on stone or ice, some roll and bounce across an urban landscape, some are comets. The beads are seeds. They sparkle and catch light. The woman is shooting marbles and planting seeds of revolution. She is playing roulette and juggling. She is planting the earth and she is planting the sky. Each bead is a cell, each cell a universe, warm spring breeze, earth—still cold and wet to the touch, sky—dark at midnight and pale blue at noon.

YOU COULD SEE A SANE FUTURE THROUGH HER EYES

Rosalie Stech Sullivan
feminist activist, civil rights activist,
peace activist

Rosalie and I walking along the gulf,
children charging the waves,
me saying, *I'm not sure there **are** any good men,*
how they're raised, arrogant, self-centered.
There are though, she told me,
and you'll find them.
And the others,
you'll find them too—
and they'll find you,
so don't lose your power,
you'll need it.

Jane and I sitting on a bench alongside the river.
Rosalie's last words were about family,
important things, how you treat people,
the sanctity of life,
children, the ones you love, who love you,
you honor life,
you honor it,
Rosalie—and Jane,
womanlight.

Rosalie and I,
walking along the gulf of Mexico.
It was January.

She'd arrived in a snow storm,
hailed a cab, and they'd stopped,
for hot toddies.
She'd been railing about something
unjust, outrageous, hysterical.
There was no interrupting her
once she got rolling.

It was a grandmother
for whom feminism was possible
that I met
the year of my divorce,
when I'd had it with America
and men
and education
and war—
and war.

I was disgusted,
as I've been since—
since Rosalie and I walked
along the Gulf of Mexico,
but I knew
someplace solid and rich,
she was right.

I could see
a sane future
through her eyes.

CURE

Let the goddess
  dance
in the sun.

She dances
  spins and draws
  a circle
  out of golden
  light
in the air above
  her as
  she moves.

If she wants
  you she will
  touch your lips
  with
  her index finger
  as she passes.

If she wants
  you
  to
  follow her
  to
  the center
  of
  your soul,

follow her,
  follow.

But only
  if the
  signal
  is
  exact.

Otherwise,
she
is
only dancing
for
herself.

PIECES OF THE LIGHT

The ancients said
we had two truths
to choose from:

   It's all in pieces.
       or
   All is one.

But now
that's wrong.
It's possible,
even likely,
that we are individual
and universal at
the exact instant
we both do and do
not exist.

So,
we can change
direction.

We
happen to be old
enough to understand.

We
happen to be free
enough to reach for it,
change.

Children line up around us.
What are we supposed to do?
What kind of world shall
we create for them?

At school,
an older boy says to a younger
child,

*I'm going to
kill you
when
we go
out to recess.*

The guide
stops everything
for a grace and courtesy lesson:

What was that you said?

The older boy
covers his face
in shame.

The guide
tells all the children:

*We do not allow the larger
children to kill the smaller
children here.*

*No one will be killed
at recess.*

You don't suppose
it is that
simple?

Tirades and Evidence of Grace is published in a first edition of 2500 copies the first 400 of which are signed and numbered.